# Traffic and Highway Engineering
## for Developments

# Traffic and Highway Engineering for Developments

**C.A. ASHLEY**
BSc, MSc, PhD, FIHT, MCIT, MBAE
Traffic/Highways Consultant

OXFORD
BLACKWELL SCIENTIFIC PUBLICATIONS
LONDON EDINBURGH BOSTON
MELBOURNE PARIS BERLIN VIENNA

© 1994 by
Blackwell Scientific Publications
Editorial Offices:
Osney Mead, Oxford OX2 0EL
25 John Street, London WC1N 2BL
23 Ainslie Place, Edinburgh EH3 6AJ
238 Main Street, Cambridge,
    Massachusetts 02142, USA
54 University Street, Carlton,
    Victoria 3053, Australia

Other Editorial Offices:
Librairie Arnette SA
1, rue de Lille
75007 Paris
France

Blackwell Wissenschafts-Verlag GmbH
Düsseldorfer Str. 38
D-10707 Berlin
Germany

Blackwell MZV
Feldgasse 13
A-1238 Wien
Austria

First published 1994

Set by DP Photosetting, Aylesbury, Bucks
Printed and bound in Great Britain by
Hartnolls Ltd, Bodmin, Cornwall

DISTRIBUTORS

Marston Book Services Ltd
PO Box 87
Oxford OX2 0DT
(*Orders:* Tel: 0865 791155
            Fax: 0865 791927
            Telex: 837515)

USA
Blackwell Scientific Publications, Inc.
238 Main Street
Cambridge, MA 02142
(*Orders:* Tel: 800 759-6102
            617 876 7000)

Canada
Oxford University Press
70 Wynford Drive
Don Mills
Ontario M3C 1J9
(*Orders:* Tel: (416) 441-2941)

Australia
Blackwell Scientific Publications Pty Ltd
54 University Street
Carlton, Victoria 3053
(*Orders:* Tel: 03 347-5552)

British Library
Cataloguing in Publication Data

A catalogue record for this book is available from
the British Library

ISBN 0–632–03613–3

Library of Congress
Cataloging in Publication Data
Ashley, Carol.
    Traffic and highway engineering for
developments/Carol Ashley.
        p.    cm.
    Includes bibliographical references and
index.
    ISBN 0–632–03613–3
    1. Traffic engineering.   2. Highway
planning.   I. Title
HE333.A85   1994
388.3'12—dc20                    93-46810
                                    CIP

# Contents

# List of Abbreviations

| | |
|---|---|
| AADT | annual average daily traffic |
| FOSD | full overtaking sight distance |
| FTA | Freight Transport Association |
| O-D | origin-destination |
| NRTF | National Road Traffic Forecasts |
| GDP | gross domestic product |
| GFA | gross floor area |
| OTU | outstation transmission unit |
| pcu | passenger car unit |
| RFC | ratio of demand traffic flow to capacity |
| SSD | stopping sight distance |
| TIA | traffic impact assessment |
| TPP | Transport Policies and Programmes |
| TRL | Transport Research Laboratory |
| TRO | Traffic Regulation Order |
| TSG | Transport Supplementary Grant |
| UTC | urban traffic control |

# Chapter 1
# Introduction

Most development proposals of any significance require planning permission, and highway matters are material in determining planning applications. It is important therefore to the success of a development that the associated traffic and highway matters are properly addressed. The access arrangements are critical in this regard, as are other traffic matters, such as car parking and servicing arrangements.

Relevant matters can range from the simple to very complex. This book aims to provide a convenient reference for factual information, from a variety of source documents, accompanied by practical guidance to assist interpretation and application. Wherever possible, data are summarized in tabular form.

However, the aim is not to just provide a series of tables and lists of factual information. Much development has taken place over the years, notably during the 1980s. For many sites which are now available for development, there is not a straightforward 'textbook' solution to all associated highway matters. In many cases the interpretation of information and application of judgement is critical in identifying the preferred approach to highways aspects of a development. Thus, within this book examples are quoted by way of explanation of a point being made. These are not meant to be (and cannot be) exhaustive, but are included to relate to a similar situation familiar to the reader, or one that the reader may encounter in the future.

A wide variety of professions, including for example architects, chartered surveyors, town planners and traffic and highway engineers, need to consider traffic and highway engineering issues in respect of developments. There can be considerable variation between professions in the underlying level of specialist highways knowledge. This therefore poses a challenge in selection and presentation of material for this book. In general terms, a comprehensive coverage of issues has been adopted, rather than a restricted selection of topics. All matters contained within the book's chapters are relevant in respect of developments, but each is not relevant to all developments.

Traffic and highways data and requirements can be subject to interpretation and professional judgement and knowledge of a wide variety of information and situations is useful. In such cases, where there may be professional disagreement between the developer's team and the highway authority, the discussions can become very detailed and highly technical in content. The advice of an experienced highways professional is required in such circumstances. However, other professions will frequently be involved and will find it most helpful to have some knowledge and understanding of the issues raised and of the relevant data.

Some of the technical detail included in this book may be at the edge of mainstream interest to some professions. However, one of the aims of this book is to provide a firm foundation for understanding the principles adopted by traffic and highway engineers when devising and considering proposals for access and other traffic matters. Thus, the intention is to assist the non-engineer to proceed with reasonable confidence in matters of simple, uncomplicated highway design requirements, as well as to provide a sound basis for appreciating when expert engineering advice is essential. In the latter case, this book should assist the non-engineer in understanding the relevance of what is proposed by the engineering adviser.

Traffic and highway engineers may use jargon and technical terms which are unfamiliar to those of other professions. This book aims to assist the reader through an explanation of such terms, so that the principles underlying the practice can better be understood. Nevertheless, some chapters do include equations and numerical treatment, thereby providing a fuller explanation of the design process. Whilst this is likely to be of most interest to traffic and highway engineers, it also offers a basis for other professions to understand the thrust of detailed technical discussions with traffic and highway engineers.

This book is not intended as a detailed design manual, nor can it be a substitute for professional experience. However, it does aim to provide practical guidance for many circumstances which can be encountered.

The Department of Transport publish design standards for trunk roads, and these are amended and replaced from time to time; the most recent advice should always be followed. Local authorities generally adopt the Department of Transport design standards as the basis of their own standards. Additionally, it is common for local authorities to adopt their own design standards in respect of specific issues, for example car parking space requirements, design of residential roads and of industrial roads. Such standards vary in detail between authorities, and not all authorities publish such advice. It is therefore essential to establish what design standards are adopted within a local authority and to understand the basis upon which these were derived.

The greater proportion of this book relates to private car and service vehicle traffic. This is because, for most developments, such traffic tends to have the greatest impact in relation to the existing situation. However, it is stressed that the traffic issues in respect of other road users: public transport, pedestrians, cyclists and disabled (mobility impaired) should be given careful and appropriate consideration for a proposed development. Although these matters are addressed in specific chapters within this book (Chapter 11 Public Transport, Chapter 12 Other Traffic), this most definitely does not imply that they are peripheral issues to be addressed in a perfunctory manner. Rather, the needs of these road users should be an integral part of the highways considerations for a development, and considered at the early stages of preparing development access strategy and traffic proposals. The issues addressed by most other chapters, (for example, roundabouts, traffic signals, car parking, service vehicles) should include appropriate consideration of the needs of public transport, pedestrians, cyclists and disabled.

It is widely acknowledged that the access arrangements for a development are crucial to its success. This is in terms of achieving a planning permission and, as important, in realizing the commercial potential of a development scheme. Where access issues are addressed at the inception of a development proposal this generally results in a more economic outcome: in terms of capital costs and fee costs of professional advisers, as well as in timescale of project progress.

# Chapter 2
# Site Access Strategy

## Aims and objectives

All developments should provide satisfactory vehicular access arrangements for traffic generated by the site. This is:

- in the interests of highway safety
- to ensure that vehicle delays are not excessive
- to promote the commercial success of the development.

In the broadest sense, 'traffic' covers the spectrum of modes, from the different categories of motorized vehicular traffic (cars, goods/service/emergency vehicles, buses, motorcycles) through non-motorized vehicles (pedal cycles) to pedestrians. A well designed development proposal takes full account of all these.

Whatever the location or scale of development, at some point the vehicular traffic travelling to and from the development will select a specific route on the existing highway network; it is essential this can be accommodated in an acceptable manner. In general, the traffic impact of a development tends to be most critical at junctions (see Chapters 7, 8 and 9). Usually a junction affords the primary development access; this may be an entirely new junction (purpose designed) or may be an existing junction (improved as necessary).

In some cases the volume of traffic generated onto the local highway network is so great that the capacity of existing highway links (see Chapter 6) may be exceeded; in such circumstances measures must be introduced to avoid this, for example by providing additional traffic lanes. Generally this problem relates to large-scale developments, for example a major business park or an out-of-town regional shopping centre.

The access strategy proposed for a development should take account of the following:

- existing traffic (prior to development) on the highway network (see Chapter 5);

to which will be added the

4

- generated traffic (net additional) – the volume and distribution (both by time and spatially) must be considered (see Chapter 5);
- mix of traffic and conflicts – for example, cars, goods/service vehicles, pedestrians, buses (see Chapters 11, 12 and 15);
- geometry of the existing highway network and relevant highway design standards (see Chapter 6);
- existing junctions in the vicinity of the development site – control, layout, capacity (see Chapters 7–9);
- safety (see Chapter 10);
- specific access requirements, for example emergency access, public transport (see Chapter 11);
- land ownerships – generally, only land under the control of the developer and/or highway land should be considered as available in respect of providing site access, (to avoid a 'ransom' situation for the developer).

The aim is to provide the most economical means of site access consistent with highway safety, but with sufficient capacity to accommodate the estimated traffic demand in an acceptable operational manner. Overdesign of junctions and/or highway links is not desirable, either in terms of financial cost or environmental impact. (An 'overdesigned' junction would provide significantly greater capacity than the expected traffic demand; this would probably involve geometry being larger than is necessary.)

Conversely, it is not in the interests of the highway authority (and hence the community in general) to approve a development proposal with access arrangements of insufficient capacity to accommodate traffic demands. Equally, it is not in the interests of the developer to propose such access arrangements, as this will not be attractive to potential purchasers or tenants of the development.

## Who benefits?

A well conceived access strategy for a development can present an opportunity to maximize the effectiveness of the development and to do so within the context of existing land uses where the development site is situated.

Consideration should be given to the policies and aspirations of the local authority in respect of different modes of transport. For example, it may be possible to include elements within the development proposal which help further the council's transport objectives, to the benefit of the community and the success of the development.

An example of this might be a major shopping development scheme which includes proposals to extend an existing light rail/tram network to serve the development. This assists the council's aspirations to encourage the use of public transport. Further, this provides convenient access to the development for those without private transport, providing increased opportunity in terms of employment and general availability of the development facilities. The effects are similar in considering provision of bus services included as part of a development proposal.

In summary, everyone benefits from a well designed development site access strategy – the community in general as well as the developer.

## Land use

The nature of the development may well have some influence on the optimal access strategy. Some types of development require a high profile access with frontage onto a major highway, (for example, a food superstore or business park), whilst other developments are not so sensitive in this sense, (for example, an exclusive residential development or a nursing home).

The context of land use within which the development site is located may influence the access strategy. For example, it is not desirable to generate significant numbers of goods vehicles along residential streets throughout the 24-hour period. Thus especial consideration must be given to access locations for developments which may have such patterns of traffic generation, for example, a manufacturing development or a regional distribution centre.

The site use prior to implementation of the proposed development is an important consideration. For example, consider a site with existing manufacturing/industrial use which has several site access points onto the adjacent residential street network where a change of use to a retail foodstore is proposed. The existing use may generate a significant number of goods vehicles onto the local residential street network. The proposed retail foodstore use will generate significantly fewer goods vehicles, representing a benefit for local residents, (albeit not a complete removal of goods vehicle movements generated by the site). Furthermore, the car traffic generated by the foodstore will be concentrated at a single, well designed site access location.

## Land ownership

A developer is most unwise to propose site access arrangements on land over which he has no control. If he does so, the developer is then in a 'ransom' situation. In general, the exception to this is highway land, in which case it would normally be made available for the undertaking of highway improvement works, without a charge being levied for the land;

this should of course be checked and confirmed with the highway authority prior to submission of a planning application.

## Emergency access

The access strategy proposed for a development should include consideration of emergency access requirements. This not only refers to emergency vehicles (such as fire, ambulance), but also to an emergency situation when normal access arrangements are in some way disrupted, such as in the case of a sewer collapse.

For example, some local authorities stipulate that residential developments should have a maximum length of cul-de-sac, for an emergency situation. Various options are available for addressing this issue, and this matter should be considered when developing the site access strategy.

## Summary

Site access strategy should ideally be considered at the inception of a development proposal. This approach offers the most cost effective way of considering the traffic/highways aspects of a development and provides the best opportunity for minimizing:

- professional fees
- time taken to develop the planning application proposal
- cost of works to enable the scheme.

# Chapter 3
# The Planning System and Highway Matters

## Planning system and development

There is a fundamental link between land use and transportation; people undertake journeys in pursuit of an activity, whether it is work, leisure, shopping or other purposes; in other words, journeys are movements between land uses. The spatial distribution of different land uses over an area has a significant effect upon the travel patterns of the population. The emphasis placed by government guidance upon the location and juxtaposition of different land uses has varied over time.

The control of development is administered by central government and local authorities, within the bounds of the 'planning system'. The procedure to be adopted in respect of planning for development is laid down by legislation. This has a history of change, at varying rates, both in emphasis and apparent intent. The late 1980s and early 1990s have seen a procession of changing legislation and government guidance to professionals. Changes may well continue to occur. The organization of the planning system is linked to the structure of local government, with an overall leading role retained by central government. Changes in organization of local government are likely to have associated effects upon the planning system.

At the level of central government, the present arrangements in England are, broadly speaking, that the Department of the Environment has responsibility for the planning system in respect of land use and the Department of Transport is responsible for matters specifically relating to transport, such as the planning and construction of trunk roads and motorways, and road and vehicle safety. (In Wales, the Welsh Office oversees both land use and transport planning.)

## Transport Policies and Programmes (TPP)

Local highway authorities in England must publish annually a document known as the *Transport Policies and Programmes* (TPP). This is a statement of the transport policies, together with a costed programme to implement these policies, using financial guidelines set down by central

8

government. The present requirement outside of London is for county councils and metropolitan councils to produce TPPs. (London boroughs and the Common Council of the City of London must also produce TPPs.) An annual circular sets out the information which should be provided in the TPP, this typically including:

(1) policies and objectives of transport planning in the county (or relevant body of authority required to publish TPP),
(2) rolling programme for the implementation of these policies,
(3) details of past progress and expenditure together with the degree to which the stated objectives are being achieved,
(4) costed proposals for the coming year.

The idea is that the local authority thus formulates a comprehensive transport plan for resource allocation, promoting operational measures and maintaining flexibility between modes. However, in practice, other policies of central government may influence the ability of the local authority to achieve the identified goals. Nevertheless, the TPP does provide an indication of those transport schemes which it is the intention of the authority to promote, and further supplies some indication of the relative importance of timescale attributed to the identified schemes. The TPP is therefore one source to check for possible future highway proposals which may affect a particular location.

The TPP is not a statutory document requiring ministerial approval, but it does represent a policy document of the local authority. The TPP is submitted to the Department of Transport (appropriate regional office) each July. The TPP includes bids (to the Department of Transport) for Transport Supplementary Grant (TSG), to provide finance for schemes which are eligible for TSG award. On the basis of the approved level of expenditure, the Department of Transport allocates its TSG, which the authority can then use to implement the proposals which have gained financial support. The TSG allocation affects the proposed timescale of implementation of projects included in the TPP; it is not usual for a local authority to be awarded the full amount of TSG which is requested.

## Planning application

Planning permission is generally required for a development proposal where change of use and/or new construction is involved. Means of access is normally a material consideration in deciding a planning application.

The highway authority considers the traffic impact of the proposed development. It needs to be satisfied that this is not likely to give rise to an unacceptable deterioration in the operational performance of the highway network and/or detriment to highway safety. The local planning authority may thus require the applicant to submit quantitative traffic information with the planning application; this can be quite detailed in some cases.

The first matter to be determined is whether the proposed development involves a change of use and/or new construction such that planning permission is required. If so, a planning application must be submitted to the local authority.

A planning application may be either *outline* or *full*. In the case of an outline planning application a number of issues may be treated as 'reserved matters', that is, reserved for agreement at a later date, (following the grant of outline planning permission). These may include, for example, the detail site layout of structures and car parking, finishes of buildings, and landscaping. An application for approval of 'reserved matters' must be submitted within three years of the date of grant of outline planning permission. The development must start either within five years of the grant of outline planning permission or within two years of final approval of 'reserved matters'.

Alternatively, if the details of the development proposal are fixed, a full application may be submitted at the outset (no submission of outline application). This approach is not suitable for the early stages of developing a scheme; for example, for a mixed use development when the precise mix of land use tenants is not confirmed at the time of submitting the planning application.

While with an outline application a number of matters may be reserved, it is commonplace that the highway authority requires the details of means of access to be demonstrated with the outline application. In this way, the local authority can guard against the situation arising where, following grant of outline planning permission, traffic/highway matters come to light which prejudice the development of access proposals that are wholly satisfactory to the authority. Thus, it is usual that even with an outline application traffic matters must be addressed in a detailed manner by the applicant, and in significantly greater detail than is required for many other aspects of the outline planning application.

## Planning conditions

The decision of a planning authority to grant permission for a development may be conditional. Conditions can relate to a variety of issues, and traffic-related matters are frequently the subject of a planning condition(s). For example, where highway works form part of the development proposal, there may be a planning condition linking the timing of the development, either construction works and/or occupation of the development, to the completion of such highway works.

It is commonplace for a developer to agree to finance infrastructure works outside the development site (off-site highway works), where it is predicted that the development will significantly contribute to an adverse effect upon operation and/or highway safety of junctions/highway links located outside the site.

When traffic/highway related works are proposed (as part of the development scheme), it is common practice for the planning permission to be conditional upon the developer entering into a legal agreement with the local authority. Such agreements may involve, for example, off-site highway improvements to assist/provide access to the site, the adoption of on-site roads or the provision of non-operational car parking outside the site boundary.

There are several ways in which the required legal agreement can be effected. The most usual approaches include the following:

*Planning Obligations Section 106, Town and Country Planning Act 1990, as amended by the Planning and Compensation Act 1991*
Obligations may be either bilateral (between the local planning authority and the developer) or unilateral (by the developer alone). The former is used where there is agreement between the two parties. The latter may be used where the Secretary of State or his Inspector is prepared to grant permission but wishes to ensure that some planning obligation to it (for example, lack of adequate off-site infrastructure) can be overcome. If the local planning authority are not prepared to enter into an agreement with the developer, then a unilateral obligation can be provided to secure the planning permission. Obligations may require the developer to carry out and/or finance specified works, or to make some other provision on land either inside or outside the application site boundary.

*Section 278 Agreement, Highways Act 1980*
Agreement between the developer and the highway authority. Where there is a proposal by the highway authority to undertake road works, the developer may agree to finance works which are additional to and/or in modification of the authority's proposed works, so that the traffic impact of the development can be minimized. Alternatively, or additionally, there may be a financial contribution from the developer to enable the 'bringing forward' in time of works proposed by the authority, thereby assisting the development to proceed.

*Section 38, Highways Act 1980*
Agreement between the developer and the highway authority. The highway authority agrees to adopt roads and footpaths constructed as part of the development, these to be maintained at public expense. The works must be designed and constructed to standards approved by the highway authority.

## Planning appeals

The developer may appeal against the decision of the planning authority, either against a refusal decision or against a planning condition(s) attached to a permission. An appeal can also be lodged if the local planning authority fail to determine an application within the statutory eight week period. Circumstances may occur where a highways condition attached to the planning consent is considered unreasonable by the applicant. An example of this might be that all off-site highway works (forming part of the development proposal) must be completed prior to commencement of construction work on the development site. The applicant may appeal against a planning condition, on grounds of unreasonableness.

Written notice of the appeal must be given to the planning inspectorate within six months of the date of the decision notice. The planning inspectorate (on behalf of the Secretary of State) appoints an independent inspector to deal with the appeal.

The appellant can request that the appeal is dealt with in one of three ways:

(1) *Written representations.* The appellant and the local planning authority each provide the inspector with written documentation in support of their respective views on the matter. There is no hearing involved.

(2) *Informal hearing.* The hearing is chaired by the inspector and both the appellant and local authority are represented. There is opportunity, at the discretion of and under the direction of the inspector, for oral statement of case by both the appellant and the local authority. The inspector may elect to permit third parties to speak. This forum is not intended to be appropriate when a significant number of the public wish to be present and/or to be heard.

(3) *Public inquiry.* This is chaired by the inspector. The appellant and local authority are required to present written and oral evidence in support of their respective cases. The public are fully entitled to attend and submit evidence at the proceedings. For a major public inquiry it is common for a barrister to present the case and to undertake the cross examination of those giving evidence. Whilst appointment of an advocate is not a requirement, for an expert witness to present objective evidence can be incompatible with conducting the case on behalf of an interested party; this view is shared by the British Academy of Experts. Frequently, a solicitor will act as advocate.

The inspector always visits the appeal site. If the site can be conveniently viewed from the road, the inspector may make an unaccompanied visit. In all other cases, irrespective of the way in which the appeal is being dealt with (written representations, informal hearing or public inquiry), the inspector visits the site accompanied by representatives of the appellant and the local planning authority.

The inspector considers all the evidence presented, and his own observations, and prepares an appeal report and recommendation. The Secretary of State considers this and confirms, or otherwise, the recommendation of the inspector. This decision is then notified to the involved parties. The time taken for the appellant to receive the appeal decision varies, depending upon a number of factors; this may, for example vary between some three weeks and 12 months.

## Checklist

### Planning application
- Is a planning application necessary for the proposed development?
- If yes, is the application to be outline or full?

### Planning conditions
- Prior to the submission of the planning application, and while this is being considered by the highway authority, discuss the nature of any traffic-related conditions which may be attached to a planning consent.
- In the event of gaining a planning permission with traffic-related conditions, consider the reasonableness of the conditions, particularly where these have not been previously agreed by the developer (or his professional adviser).
- If a condition relating to traffic/highways matters imposed on the planning consent is considered by the applicant to be unreasonable, an appeal can be made against such conditions.

### Planning appeals against refusal of consent
- Decide whether to appeal to the Department of the Environment against the refusal of planning consent.
- Decide the desired form of appeal to be pursued: written representations, informal hearing or public inquiry.
- Within six months of the refusal decision date give written notice of the intention to appeal.

# Chapter 4
# Traffic Impact Assessment

## Need for a traffic impact assessment (TIA)

The planning authority requests the views of the highway authority in respect of a planning application; the highway authority requires appropriate information as the basis for determining its views. A traffic impact assessment (TIA) study addresses the range of issues relevant to the traffic/highway aspects of a development proposal. Although there is not a statutory requirement to submit a TIA in support of a planning application, this is increasingly requested by planning authorities (for proposed developments which may have a significant impact on the highway network).

A primary objective of the TIA is to provide relevant supporting information for a planning application, so that the highway authority can be satisfied as to the acceptability of the traffic impact of the proposed development. The findings of the TIA study are usually presented in a report; this can be a convenient form in which to provide the traffic/highways information required to support a planning application.

Ideally, the TIA is undertaken prior to submission of a planning application. However, where this procedure is not followed it may become necessary to subsequently undertake a TIA, either before the application is determined or in preparation for a planning appeal. Other circumstances occur in which a TIA may be undertaken following submission of a planning application: for example, when there is dispute involving third parties (other than the highway authority and applicant), over the traffic impact of a proposed development. In such circumstances a third party may commission a TIA to consider issues which they consider inadequately or inappropriately addressed by the applicant and/or the highway authority.

The precise form of a TIA can vary between projects, with the relative importance of specific issues influenced by a number of factors, including proposed development use and context of site location. However, over the years, a general consensus has emerged of issues which should be addressed by a TIA. It should be noted that this 'addressing of issues' may simply result in recognition that, for a specific development proposal, some issues do not require actions. For example, it may be concluded that there is no significant impact upon public transport provision as a consequence of the proposed development, or that similarly analysis of operational performance of junctions is not required since the levels of traffic are low.

*TIA Guidelines*, to be published by the Institution of Highways and Transportation in 1994, is intended to represent a guide to current good practice and explicitly not to be prescriptive. It is not desirable, nor is there a need, to adopt a rigid approach to preparation of a TIA report. Similarly, no single methodology is appropriate in all circumstances; for example, in respect of estimating the traffic generated by a development, or in estimating the distribution onto the highway network of the development traffic. Succeeding chapters within this text address specific issues which should be considered in respect of a TIA.

## Extent of TIA study: scoping study

It is desirable that for a proposed development the required extent and scope of TIA is agreed between the highway authority and the developer at the earliest opportunity and at the early stages of considering or preparing a planning application. In this way both parties are best assured of the most efficient allocation of time and resources expended in considering the traffic impact of the proposed development. It is in the interests of both the highway authority and the developer that assessment of the traffic impact of the development is undertaken prior to submission of the planning application.

The *TIA Guidelines* (of the Institution of Highways and Transportation) have defined the term 'scoping study' to describe this practice of early agreement (between the highway authority and developer) of the extent of TIA required. It is recommended that a scoping study should be standard good practice.

It may arise, however, that the required extent and scope of TIA does not become wholly clear until some initial results of analysis are available. Therefore, it may be necessary to consider a staged approach to definition of the required extent of TIA.

In some cases the TIA may only need to consider the junction providing direct site access and exit. In others, it may be necessary to consider the traffic impacts of the development over a wider geographical area. This depends upon a variety of features, including the existing traffic flows and highway network as well as the scale of development proposed.

## Agreement of data: highway authority and developer

It is sensible practice for the developer's representatives to discuss with the highway authority the traffic/highways aspects of the development proposal in the course of undertaking the TIA, (and whilst the planning application is being prepared). It is in the interests of both the developer and highway authority parties to agree as much technical data as possible, at the earliest opportunity. In this way, any points of disagreement which may exist between highways professionals acting for the developer and those acting for the highway authority can be identified and restricted to a minimum (ideally there being no points of disagreement). This is helpful for the highway authority officers when considering the TIA report and also for an inspector, should there to be a subsequent appeal against refusal of planning permission.

## Content of TIA report

The detailed format of the TIA report varies depending upon the nature of the development proposal and the complexity of the associated traffic issues. For example, a TIA report for a major development may include the following chapters:

- Introduction
- Highway network
- Traffic flows
- Traffic generation/attraction
- Site access arrangements
- Car parking and servicing arrangements*
- Traffic and highway related works
- Operational performance of highway network
- Public transport*
- Pedestrians*
- Pedal cyclists*
- Highway safety
- Conclusions.

*Note:* *These issues may often be satisfactorily addressed in the chapter 'Site access arrangements'.

Generally, several of the above may be conveniently combined if the issues are comparatively straightforward. Production of an over-lengthy repetitive TIA report is not in the interests of any party. The objective should be to clearly and succinctly include an assessment of all relevant issues. There follows a brief indication of the relevant matter which might be included.

### Introduction

This sets out the background to the study and the parameters of the assessment. The development site can be conveniently identified by including a suitable location plan. The extent of the study area or study length is defined for the purposes of the TIA, preferably having been previously agreed with the highway authority.

## Highway network

The existing highway network in the area of the site is described. Relevant features to be identified for the defined study area or length may include: road names, speed restrictions, carriageway details (width, central reservations, pedestrian refuges, etc.), parking restrictions, one-way operation, turning restrictions, mandatory manoeuvres, location of junctions and accesses, pedestrian facilities, and other significant features. The form of operation is described for junctions which are of significance in the context of the study.

Any committed or planned highway schemes which affect the study area should be identified, together with information in respect of programming.

## Traffic flows

The traffic flows which occur in the 'No Development' scenario must be established for the existing situation and estimated for the proposed development year of opening and, if appropriate, for a 'future design year'. This applies to the time periods of greatest traffic impact of the development. This is discussed later in Chapter 5.

## Traffic generation/attraction

Similarly, the information relevant to the TIA report chapter 'Traffic generation/attraction' is discussed in Chapter 5. Quantitative assessment is required of the traffic generated and attracted by the proposed development and the consequent net additional traffic generated onto the local highway network. The likely distribution onto the highway network of the development traffic must also be considered.

## Site access arrangements

The proposed site access arrangements are usually best explained with the assistance of a plan and diagrams. The nature of proposed junction controls should be clearly identified.

## Car parking and servicing arrangements

It may be that car parking and service access arrangements can be included within 'Site access arrangements', and that separate individual chapters are not required to deal with these issues. This depends very much upon the nature and detail of the development project. Chapters 14 and 15 consider the matters of car parking and service vehicles respectively.

### Traffic and highway related works

The nature and extent of the traffic management and highway works proposed as part of the development should be explicitly described. A clear plan illustrating these measures is most helpful. It may be that these matters can be conveniently described in 'Site access arrangements'. Chapters 6–9 consider the design aspects of highway links and different forms of junction control; Chapter 13 describes other traffic management measures which may be included as part of a development proposal.

### Operational performance of the highway network

The methodology of analysis adopted for the study should be defined. The techniques and tools available for analysing the predicted performance of different forms of junction control are described in Chapters 7–9.

The analysis findings should be summarized in a manner that is easily understood; tables and diagrams may be used. However, it is not generally appropriate or helpful to include pages of computer printout within the report; the highway authority can request such output separately if they require it. In general, this can be avoided if well planned summary tables are presented. Tables summarizing the results of analysis should be complemented by a clear explanation of interpretation.

In some few cases of very large-scale developments it may be considered appropriate to undertake area-wide modelling of the performance of the highway network, using a traffic model incorporating a traffic assignment technique, (for example, equilibrium assignment, congested assignment or other). There are a number of proprietary computer packages available for such analysis, for example SATURN, TRIPS, QVIEW; each of these employs a different mathematical basis for assigning traffic to a congested highway network. In the absence of an available suitably calibrated traffic model, it is necessary to 'build' such a computer traffic model for the defined study area. This can be costly, and for this reason caution is recommended in deciding to adopt this method of analytical approach.

However, the local authority may have a traffic model available which includes the area of the development proposal. In such cases the highway authority may agree to undertake analysis on behalf of the applicant. However, this approach does limit the scope for the professional advisors of the developer to be fully assured of the appropriateness of the traffic model (both in terms of input and analysis technique) and hence the output may not necessarily be agreed. The approach of using an area-wide traffic model of this type for the purposes of the TIA is not discussed further, as for such work professional traffic modelling expertise is essential, and details are considered to lie outside this book's objectives.

### Public transport

This chapter considers aspects of public transport provision relevant to the development. This may most commonly apply to buses, but also includes other services, for example, rail and tram systems. Public transport issues are discussed in Chapter 11.

### Pedestrians

The provision for pedestrians, both in and on the approaches to the development site, may require explicit description within the separate report chapter 'Pedestrians', or may be dealt with in other chapters, for example, 'Site access arrangements'. The scope and scale of pedestrian provision relating to the development scheme proposal determines the appropriate approach within the report. Chapter 12 considers some general matters relating to pedestrian needs and provision of facilities. Chapter 13 considers aspects of pedestrianization schemes.

### (Pedal) cyclists

Depending upon the location of the site and the policy of the local authority, it may be appropriate to include a report chapter 'Cyclists'. This depends upon whether any elements of the development proposal affect cyclists, either in terms of introducing or improving cyclist facilities or detrimental effects. Again, it may be that this issue can be satisfactorily addressed in the Chapter 'Site access arrangements'. Chapter 12 discusses some aspects of cyclist needs and facilities.

### Highway safety

This chapter may be explicitly included if the subject has not been dealt with in sufficient detail in the preceding parts of the report. Chapter 10 considers aspects of road safety.

### Conclusions

This should set out clearly and succinctly the main points arising from the TIA, providing an 'at a glance' summary of the salient elements of the development proposals (in traffic/highway terms) and the reporting of the analysis findings.

It may well be that for a public inquiry this chapter can form the basis of the summary (of proof of evidence) that is required to be submitted.

## Checklist

- Define study area.
- Scoping study: identify issues to be addressed, e.g. extent of study area, traffic generation, performance of junctions, car parking, servicing, pedestrians, public transport, cyclists, road safety.
- Ascertain whether there are any highway schemes proposed by the local authority, or others, which may affect the study network; TPP is one source to check (see Chapter 3).
- Define proposed access arrangements for development.
- Define time periods for analysis of traffic impact (see Chapter 5).
- Obtain necessary traffic flow data; either purchase, if available, or undertake traffic surveys (see Chapter 5).
- Define appropriate years for analysis of traffic impact; factor traffic flows as required (see Chapter 5).
- Estimate traffic generated/attracted by development; estimate net additional traffic (see Chapter 5).
- Define distribution of traffic onto the highway network, for analysis purposes (see Chapter 5).
- Analyse quantitatively the operational performance of the study network (see Chapters 7–9).
- Prepare report summarizing the TIA.
- Always discuss and agree with the highway authority, in the course of the study, as much data as possible.

# Chapter 5
# Traffic Flows

## General

It is appreciated that to those who do not come from a traffic or highway engineering profession, traffic flows may not hold immediate interest. However, when the traffic impact of a proposed development is significant, this is material for determining a planning application (or appeal). Traffic flows are *fundamental* to the assessment of traffic impact of a proposed development. Relevant issues include:

- traffic *generated/attracted* by the proposed development (gross traffic movements, as well as net additional traffic);
- *distribution* onto highway network of traffic generated by proposed development;
- *existing* traffic flows on highway network;
- *future* year traffic flows predicted on the highway network (assuming the proposed development does not occur).

There are a variety of circumstances for which the traffic impact of a development may be significant. Inconveniently, it is not possible to draw up a list covering all such situations. In some cases the volume of generated traffic may be so great that the traffic impact should be thoroughly investigated as a matter of course, in others the generated traffic volume may be low (say, one or two peak hour vehicles) but considered to be significant in the context of the existing highway conditions. Thus, it is not always the case that large volumes of generated traffic necessitate highway improvement works, nor conversely that relatively low volumes of traffic can always be accommodated in an acceptable manner by the existing highway network. Rather, this depends upon a number of factors, including the spare capacity available within the highway network in relation to the volume of generated/attracted traffic, as well as the overall context of existing conditions onto which the development traffic is superimposed. It is this uncertainty in respect of assessing the traffic impact of a proposal that prompts the need to undertake a traffic impact assessment (*see* Chapter 4) for many developments and traffic flows (existing and development generated) are central to this.

For example, when the existing highway network is heavily congested even a small increase in traffic flows at a critical junction may be considered unacceptable without highway improvements to the junction. Another example of significant traffic impact is where the highway network is adequate to accommodate existing traffic flows (up to and including the traffic growth predicted for a future design year), but the proposed development generates large additional volumes of traffic which cannot also be accommodated without highway improvements to the highway network.

The issues outlined above are now considered in more detail.

## Traffic generation/attraction

### Development land use

In the classical terminology of transportation planning, land uses are defined as either trip generators or trip attractors. Trip generators are residential use and trip attractors are uses which attract people, for journey purposes such as work, education, shopping, leisure and so on. However, within the context of considering the traffic impact of developments, it is common practice to refer to 'traffic generation of the proposed development use', irrespective of the nature of use. That convention is adopted within this book: traffic generated or attracted by a development use is henceforth referred to as 'generated traffic' and is defined as traffic travelling to and from the development.

The traffic generated by a site is dependent upon the particular uses present. The planning system has a use classification system which is defined in the Town and Country Planning Use Classes Order 1987. However, for the purposes of estimating the trip generation profile of a proposed development, it is general practice to consider the use 'classification' in relation to the trip generation characteristics, so that traffic generation can be estimated with some reasonable confidence. Categories commonly referred to in respect of traffic generation include:

- residential
- food retail
- non-food retail
- offices
- leisure (e.g. bowling alley, multi-screen cinema)
- fast food and restaurants
- hotel and conference centres
- petrol filling stations.

The development uses listed above exhibit different patterns of trip generation, both in terms of volume and distribution in time. These may have 'sub-categories' in terms of trip generation, by virtue of the differing trip generating characteristics ascribing to each. For example:

- food retail, may be food superstore or discount foodstore;
- non-food retail, may be a discrete store with or without garden centre, or a retail park;
- office, may be a discrete town centre building or a business park.

In each of the above examples the vehicle trip generation rate is different for the alternative sub-categories cited.

## Time periods

The time periods for which traffic generation estimates may be required depend in part upon the nature of the proposed use (and the associated peak periods of trip generation) and in part upon the time of existing peak traffic demand on the highway network. Time periods to be analysed may include:

- weekday peak hours: morning and/or evening
- Saturday peak hour
- daily.

Consider the weekday evening: 1700–1800 hours is typically the peak hour of traffic generation for many proposed development uses, including for example, offices, residential and food retail. Commonly, this is also the evening peak hour for existing traffic flow on the highway network. Therefore, for many development uses the appropriate weekday evening peak period for assessing maximum traffic impact is typically 1700–1800 hours. For example, for a food superstore the Friday evening is generally the 'worst case' weekday period (maximum traffic generation) with 1700–1800 hours representing the peak hour for store arrivals and departures as well as the time of maximum existing traffic flow on the highway network.

Similarly, for development uses which also generate significant weekday morning peak hour trips, such as offices and residential, the appropriate morning time period for assessing maximum development impact is typically 0800–0900 hours.

Saturday traffic may be critical in respect of some developments. Hence it can be necessary to examine the traffic impact of the development for that day. An example where this might arise is in a major town centre retail development. The peak hour for development traffic impact must be defined for the purpose of analysis. For the example given, the peak hour may be 1300–1400 hours, although there may well be a similar level of traffic flow over several hours in the central part of the Saturday.

The daily trip generation estimate may be required in some cases. This may apply, for example, in the case of assessing the daily capacity of a highway link, such as a new bypass.

### Trip generation rates

The traffic/highways impact of a development must be assessed in terms of the vehicular traffic generated by the development. A 'trip generation rate' is commonly used to estimate such traffic flows.

Examples of weekday trip generation rates are presented in Table 5.1. It should be noted that these are only typical examples, within a range of observations, and not definitive values which apply in all cases. These are presented only to give some indicative quantification of typical levels of trip generation.

When considering possible alternative development uses for a site, traffic generation may be a significant factor in developing a scheme proposal acceptable to the local authority. In such cases, and especially at the early stages of devising a development scheme proposal, it is useful to have some general 'feel' for the comparative trip generation of different uses (although detailed estimates will also be required at the appropriate

**Table 5.1**   Typical trip generation rates: weekday peak hours.

| Site use | Vehicles/peak hour/100 sm GFA[1] or/dwelling | | | |
| | AM | | PM | |
| | Main[2] | Contrary[3] | Main[2] | Contrary[3] |
|---|---|---|---|---|
| Offices | 2.0 | 0.5 | 0.5 | 2.0 |
| Food superstore | | | 6.1 | 6.1 |
| DIY store | | | 2.5 | 2.5 |
| Residential | 0.7 | 0.1 | 0.1 | 0.7 |

*Notes*

(1) sm = square metres
   GFA = gross floor area
   Thus, 100 sm GFA = 100 square metres gross floor area

(2) 'Main' is direction of primary flow of traffic generated by development use,
   e.g. office:       AM, main direction is arrivals;
   residential:    AM, main direction is departures.

(3) 'Contrary' is direction of secondary flow of traffic generated by development use and is opposite direction to 'Main', e.g. office: AM, contrary direction is departures.

Quoted values are indicative only; local information should be utilized where available.

time). There follow some general points which may be helpful in this regard.

Some development uses generate evening peak hour flows which are approximately the transposition of the morning peak hour flows, for example offices and residential. Of such land uses, as a general rule-of-thumb, the office use is likely to generate the highest levels of vehicular traffic for a given site.

However, some development uses generate significantly higher flows in the evening peak hour than does the office use (for a given gross floor area of development), but generate comparatively low flows in the morning peak hour. Such uses are generally retail based, a notable example being a food superstore.

### Approaches to estimating trip generation

Approaches used as the basis for estimating traffic generated by a development proposal include:

- first principles
- comparison with similar existing developments
- formulae
- complex models.

The *first principles* approach requires assumptions about the development and those using it. Consider for example the proposal for a new golf course (say in an area popular with leisure walkers). Vehicular access is proposed from a highway which carries significant levels of leisure traffic at weekends. A Saturday competition day, (with the combination of golf traffic and existing Saturday flows), may represent a significant traffic impact. In the first principles method, assumptions are made, including: time interval between competitors teeing-off, start time of competition, number of competitors, percentage of competitors arriving by private car (and percentage of those which are drivers and passengers), and so on. All this information is used to build up a vehicular trip generation profile for the competition day.

The most widely adopted practice for estimating the vehicular trips generated by developments is the *comparison* approach. Estimates of trip generation derive from data collected at existing developments. This approach is accepted by the private and public sector alike and has proved reasonably robust in a variety of situations. The trip generation rate to be adopted should take account of any special features relating to the site location and the development use. For a new development, whenever possible, it is preferable to adopt a trip generation rate which derives from data for several existing sites (which reflect similar conditions to the proposed development). In pursuance of a robust estimate, a value higher than the average trip generation rate may be used, say perhaps approximately the 85th percentile value. Where it is proposed to extend an existing development, the actual trip generation rate can be measured and used as the basis for estimating the trips generated by the proposal.

Comparatively, the *formulae* and *complex models* approaches are not widely used. The former tend to be very site specific and deriving from research-type projects. Examples of the latter are:

(1) A land use transportation model (traffic model): Use of this would generally depend upon such a model being already available, in which case the appropriateness of the model assumptions should be carefully appraised (as the model may have been developed for very different purposes).
(2) A shopping model (for a retail development proposal), which may be developed for assessing the shopping impact of a development (for example, a food superstore). The shopping model considers financial matters, which do not translate in a straightforward and reliable way to vehicle trips at specified time periods. Caution should be exercised in using shopping models alone to estimate traffic generation.

## Generated traffic new to the highway network

In general, the traffic generated by a development is *not all new* to the highway network. A primary objective of the traffic impact assessment is to consider the effect of the *increase* in traffic on the highway network which occurs as a consequence of the proposed development; this includes considering operational performance of the highway network and associated matters of highway safety. There are several issues which should be considered when estimating the net additional traffic generated by the proposed development, as this requires a quantitative estimate of those trips to and from the proposed development made by vehicles already travelling on the highway network.

### Area-wide

It is perhaps in the area-wide context, say at the level of a town (as compared with considering the roads immediately adjacent to the development site), that it is easiest to appreciate that often the traffic generated by a development is not all new to the highway network. Generally, some of the traffic generated by a development is existing traffic redistributing over the highway network as the driver destination changes.

For example, there is some evidence that food retail use generates low levels of new trips on the area-wide network. There is evidence that for 'home-store-home' car shopping trips to a new food superstore, the proportion of newly generated trips is zero, or very close to it, when there are a number of competing stores. In other words, the home-store-home shopping trips made to the new food superstore were previously made to another store, and are thus vehicular shopping trips redistributed over the area-wide highway network. Similarly, a very high percentage of 'work-store-home' shopping trips to a new food superstore are likely to be trips redistributing over the area-wide highway network, as these shopping trips change store destination.

Another example is that of the employees at a new office development being previously located at another office building in the area.

Such traffic is already on the highway prior to opening of the new development. There may be some reassignment over the highway net-work of the existing traffic, but this traffic is *already existing on the area-wide network*.

On the other hand, a new leisure facility may generate a significant level of new trips, these not previously being made anywhere on the highway network (the development creating a new demand, for example an ice rink in a town which previously did not have one).

### Redistributed traffic on the highway network: in the vicinity of the development site

It should be noted that the traffic impact assessment requires an estima-tion of the percentage of generated trips which are not new to the highway network *in the vicinity of the development site*. This may be expected to differ from the percentage of new trips generated over the area-wide highway network.

The development generated traffic on the highway network in the vicinity of the proposed development can be either:

- *new* – not previously occurring on the highway network local to the development site, or
- *redistributed* (or *transferred*) – previously trips to competing site(s).

Trips which are not new to the highway network in the vicinity of the development site can be:

- *pass-by* trips, or
- *diverted* trips.

A pass-by trip does not require a diversion from the route that would otherwise be followed, or at least this is minimal. A diverted trip requires a significant diversion from the route that would otherwise have been taken (if the intermediate shopping stop had not been added to the journey).

There is some general agreement that a discount allowance should be applied to the generated trip estimates, for pass-by traffic that would otherwise, whether or not the proposed development proceeds, be on the local highway network. Quantification of the proportion of the development generated traffic which is not new to the local highway network (being already existing on the network) is not clearcut. However, an assessment of this is required to estimate a 'discount percentage' to be applied to the development generated traffic estimates; to avoid the analysis including 'double counting' of vehicles on the local highway network. There is not a definitive value shown to be applicable in all cases. The percentage of development generated trips which are not new network trips differs between land uses.

The greatest amount of recorded information relates to food retail use, for which it is widely accepted that typically perhaps some 30% of generated traffic is already existing on the highway network (thus some 70% of trips to and from the foodstore are new network trips). Whilst 30% is a typical overall value applied to represent the foodstore gener-ated traffic which is already on the local highway network, it is stressed that this figure should not be applied indiscriminately and especially not where there are local conditions or information which support an alter-native approach.

There are not presently available correspondingly reliable percentage figures for other development uses, and the 'discount' percentage applied to represent generated traffic already on the local highway network is always a matter for careful consideration taking account of local factors and conditions.

Unlike pass-by trips, diverted trips are more generally considered as being new to the local highway network.

### Historic site use

Another issue which must be addressed in respect of the development generated traffic which is not new to the highway network in the vicinity of the site is that of 'historic site use'. One or more of the following may apply to the site of the proposed development:

- an existing site use which generates traffic,
- a valid planning permission for a particular use (but not yet imple-mented),
- a previous site use which generated traffic and which could be reinstated without the need to apply for planning permission.

In any of the above circumstances, the traffic generated by the proposed development use should be considered in the context of traffic which is currently generated by the site and/or traffic which could be generated by permitted site use. This traffic should be deducted from the estimate of traffic generated by the proposed development, as part of the process of estimating the net additional traffic generated onto the highway network (in the vicinity of the site) by the proposed development for which planning permission is sought.

## Distribution of generated traffic

A directional distribution over the highway network must be assumed for the traffic generated by the proposed development, so that the localized traffic impact of the development can be assessed. There are a variety of 'techniques' employed for estimating this distribution of traffic, including:

- local knowledge
- distributional split of existing traffic
- traffic models
- travel isochrones
- gravity model.

Whichever approach is adopted, the assumptions should be carefully appraised. For example, note that the earlier comments about shopping models (in respect of approaches for estimating trip generation) apply equally to estimating trip distribution; the shopping model relates to financial matters which may not reliably translate to vehicle trips. Hence the shopping model distribution of customer trading is not necessarily the same as the customer vehicle trip distribution.

In some cases the estimated distribution of generated traffic can vary significantly depending upon which of the above approaches is adopted. If the performance of specific junctions and/or highway links is particularly sensitive (for example, existing congested highway network), then it may be prudent to analyse the traffic impact of the proposed development for an 'envelope' of distribution scenarios. Consider the example where there is some apparent justification for two alternative distributions, A and B:

Distribution 'A'    assumes 25% northbound, 75% southbound
Distribution 'B'    assumes 60% northbound, 40% southbound.

In such circumstances it is recommended that sensitivity testing of the traffic impact analysis is achieved by considering both of these distribution scenarios, A and B, thereby ensuring some robust confidence in the conclusions drawn, and recognizing that the actual distribution may well lie somewhere between the boundaries of the envelope of distributions analysed.

# Existing traffic

The extent of the highway network to be considered when assessing the traffic impact of a proposed development must be defined. This may range from a single junction providing sole access to a development, to a wide area of the highway network including several junctions.

A reliable estimate of the existing traffic flows on the highway network, as present without the proposed development, is required. This is usually obtained by traffic count survey. Such information may be collected on a fairly regular basis by the highway authority, for major junctions and highway link locations. If the required information is available from the highway authority, and is reasonably up-to-date, (say within three years or so of the present) then purchase is recommended. This provides a cost-effective and speedy way of acquiring the necessary information and generally ensures that the data are agreed with the highway authority.

## Traffic counts

If the required traffic count data are not available for purchase, then a survey(s) must be conducted. The method employed may be manual or automatic counting or use of video techniques.

A manual traffic count is normally adopted if accurate turning movements are required at a junction. Recording of vehicles by classification is usual. This can include many classes, as with the Department of Transport manual enumeration form which identifies 11 vehicle categories. However, for the majority of cases a simple classification will suffice, such as:

Cars  includes cars, taxis, motorcycles, light commercial vehicles (up to 1.5 tonnes unladen)

HGV  heavy goods vehicles (over 1.5 tonnes unladen; six wheels or more)

PSV  public service vehicles – buses, coaches.

Automatic counts are appropriate where continuous information is required over an extended period, for example a 24 hour, seven day count. There is a variety of equipment available. The common features are some form of detector and a recording device. A simple automatic counting system may record numbers of axle pairs in a two-way total. A more sophisticated system may record number of vehicles, classified by length, in a single direction of travel. The automatic counting method does not provide a direct record of classified turning manoeuvres.

Video camera techniques may be used to record complicated patterns of traffic movement, for example at a roundabout. Subsequently the video must be interpreted to extract the required information.

### Accuracy of traffic count data

Traffic counts are undertaken to quantify the level of traffic flow over given time periods. Once collected this is historic data. The purpose of collecting the information is to assist the quantification of existing operational performance of the highway junction or link, and to then assist in predicting the future performance under different possible conditions for example, highway improvements or predicted future traffic flows.

There is inherent variability over time in traffic flows (see 'Traffic variation', later in this chapter). Additionally, traffic flows at a given location can typically vary in some locations by about 10% on a daily basis. This can arise, for example, in the peak hour on a busy commuter route where there are reasonably attractive alternative routes. In other locations, where no attractive alternative route is available, peak hour traffic flows may be very stable from day to day.

A manual 16 hour traffic count may be considered to typically have an accuracy of $\pm 10\%$. This illustrates the point that traffic count data are not (and cannot be) absolute in accuracy for time periods being considered. Nevertheless, the information does provide an adequate basis for assessing the performance of highway junctions and links. However, traffic count data should not be imbued with an assumed accuracy which is not appropriate, and the resulting analysis should similarly be interpreted in a discerning manner.

### Counting periods

Hourly traffic count data are significant in all engineering design. Peak flows along roads or at junctions are generally used to determine the capacity that should be provided in urban areas.

The time period over which traffic count data are required depends upon the proposed development use. The information is required to enable assessment of the traffic impact of adding onto the highway network the development generated traffic, at the time when the combination of existing and generated traffic is most critical in operational terms. For example, for a proposed food superstore a Friday evening weekday traffic count between 1630 and 1830 hours may suffice; whereas for a proposed office development weekday morning and evening peak period surveys are probably required, and in some cases daily traffic flow data are needed.

Average flows throughout the year are used in the economic assessment of new or improved road and junction schemes and also for the assessment of accident statistics on a road (in relation to the accident rate per million vehicle kilometres). When 16 hour (0600–2200 hour) and annual average daily traffic (AADT) flows are required, it is acceptable in some cases to estimate these flows from short period counts (of between 4 and 12 hours). The recommended short counting periods for estimating 16 hour and AADT flows are published by the Department of Transport together with the associated average coefficients of variation (Department of Transport, 1993).

The Department of Transport also publish 'conversion factors' for estimating peak hour traffic flow from daily traffic count data (or 16 hour flow data) for different categories of road type, and conversely for estimating daily (or 16 hour flows) from peak hour traffic count data (Department of Transport, 1993).

## Origin-destination data

Sometimes, the traffic flow information required extends beyond simple quantification of vehicle flow and turning movements at a location. Quantitative data about traffic movements through and within a defined area may be needed. A survey which does this is termed an origin-destination (O-D) survey. The *study area* is defined by an *external cordon*. This is an imaginary continuous line drawn around an area.

An O-D survey identifies where trips commence (origin) and end (destination). Each recorded origin-destination trip represents a single vehicle desire manoeuvre in relation to the study area. Such information is particularly relevant when considering a traffic/highway scheme which will result in a significant reassignment of vehicle trips over the highway network. An example of this might be the proposed pedestrianization of a length of highway which presently provides a through route across an area. O-D survey data is required to develop and calibrate a computer traffic model representing the existing travel patterns. This model can then be used to predict the reassignment of traffic consequent upon the proposed traffic scheme and thus assess the traffic impact on the highway network.

An O-D survey identifies the amount of travel between various locations: that is, it shows *travel desires*. It does *not* provide details of the route taken between the origin (start) and destination (end) of the trip. The information collected enables the production of 'desire line' diagrams (see 'Presentation of data' later in this chapter).

*Cordon stations* are defined at locations where the cordon crosses highways having significant levels of traffic flow. Effectively, the cordon is drawn by connecting the cordon station locations. Directional survey data must be collected at all cordon station locations. The number of survey personnel required and the consequent cost of the survey is directly related to the number of cordon stations. It is quite usual that a cordon station is not defined at *every* location where the cordon crosses a highway. This is a practical decision to limit the personnel requirement and cost of survey. However, this does introduce into the survey some known, but unquantified, element of missing survey data. Judgement must be exercised (based upon on-site observations) when deciding which highway crossings of the cordon will not be defined as cordon stations.

The study area is divided into traffic *zones*. It is not usually convenient to consider the O-D data of individual trips collected in a survey in terms of discrete addresses. Therefore, individual geographic locations are grouped into zones identified by a numeric code. All journeys with origins, or destinations, within a zone are then assumed to begin, or end, at the zone centroid. As far as possible, zones should be defined to be of homogeneous use, so that the predominant land use within a zone is either (in classical transportation planning terminology) a trip generator (e.g. residential) or a trip attractor (e.g. retail, offices). The reason for this is that because of the zone centroid assumption, trips which have both the origin and destination within the same zone cannot be represented within the survey trip matrix.

A screenline is a line which divides the area within the external cordon (the study area). It is defined so that the trips crossing it at the time of survey can be easily measured. Screenline survey data can be used to check and extend the usefulness of the O-D cordon station data.

Tripmaking data can be conveniently classified according to the origin and destination (in relation to the study area) of the trip being considered, as summarized in Table 5.2. Figure 5.1 illustrates diagrammatically the different types of O-D trip.

### *Origin-destination survey methods*

The types of O-D survey generally conducted are:

- roadside interview
- postcard survey
- registration number survey
- household interview.

**Table 5.2** Origin-destination trip types.

| Trip type | Location relative to external cordon | |
|---|---|---|
| | Origin | Destination |
| (a) Through | Outside | Outside |
| (b) External-internal | Outside | Inside |
| (c) Internal-external | Inside | Outside |
| (d) Internal | Inside | Inside |

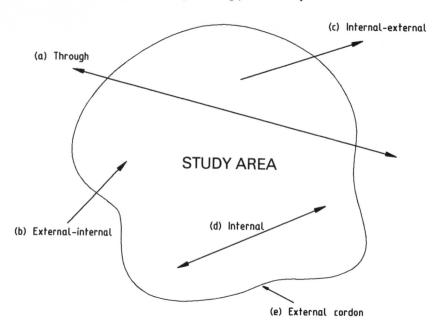

**Fig. 5.1** Types of O-D trip.

Through-trips and trips with either the origin or destination outside the external cordon (trip types (a), (b) and (c) defined in Table 5.2) are usually recorded by an O-D survey conducted along the external cordon. The roadside interview, postcard and registration number survey methods fall into this category. Internal trips, with both origin and destination inside the external cordon (trip type (d) defined in Table 5.2) are best recorded by a household interview survey.

An additional technique referred to in some textbooks is the 'vehicle tag survey', which is a variation on the registration number method. The vehicle tag survey requires a significant increase in personnel from the registration number method (consequently more costly) and introduces delay to vehicles. It does not produce data additional to that derived from a registration number survey. Therefore, the vehicle tag method is not recommended and is rarely used.

### Roadside interview

The recommended procedure for conducting a roadside interview survey is outlined in Department of Transport publications (1993 and 1981). A random sample of drivers are stopped and interviewed over the survey period (for example, weekday morning peak); journey details are recorded. With respect to representative sample size, it is the number of drivers interviewed in any one period which is the main criterion, not the proportion of total flow in that period.

A directional classified count of vehicles passing through the cordon station is carried out concurrent with undertaking motorist interviews. The traffic count must not be interrupted, even if interviews are temporarily suspended. The traffic count data are used to expand the interview sample to represent the population of motorists passing through the cordon station during the period of survey interest.

Approval is needed for conducting a roadside interview survey, as follows:

| Survey location | Approval needed from |
| --- | --- |
| Non-trunk roads | Local Highway Authority |
| Trunk road | Department of Transport |
| Motorways | Secretary of State |

### Postcard survey

Postcards are distributed to travellers for self-completion and return by reply-paid post. Features of this survey method are:

- information similar to that obtained with roadside interview, but much cheaper
- low response rate
- biased sample.

Because of the latter two features this is not a generally recommended survey method, and should only be used if there is no other viable alternative. A note of caution: be sure that the type of data obtainable (biased sample, low response rate) will suffice for the purpose for which it is being collected.

### Registration number survey

Registration numbers of vehicles crossing the external cordon are recorded simultaneously at all defined cordon stations for the whole of the survey period. The information obtained is at the locations where vehicles enter and leave the study area and these are taken as the survey origins and destinations respectively. The registration numbers are subsequently 'matched' to produce an O-D matrix for the study area over the survey period.

Vehicles are not stopped and thus no obvious disruption to vehicular flow is attributable to the survey. This is an advantage at periods of peak traffic flow. A practical point is that the survey start and finish times are usually offset to take account of the time taken to traverse the study area.

There are two alternative ways of recording the registration number:

- survey personnel positioned at cordon stations, or
- photographic (video cameras or time-lapse cameras).

The personnel technique is the more commonly adopted. At busy locations recording of the full registration number is likely not to be practical. Therefore, partial registration number data are usually recorded, commonly being the year letter and three adjacent numerals, with the character block being ignored; for example, for J234 ABC record J234, for CDE 456X record 456X. Similarly, it may not, in practice, be feasible to manually record all registration numbers. In such circumstances, some unbiased form of sampling is usually adopted (uniformly at all survey points), such as 'all registration numbers ending in an even number'. Generally, at heavily trafficked sites, portable tape recorders are needed to cope with the volume of data to be logged.

However obtained, the survey data is usually processed and analysed using a computer program, several such programs being commercially available. The manual alternative is extremely time consuming and generally results in a lower match-rate for registration numbers than if a computer program is used.

If the only data collected is at external cordon stations, it is not possible to obtain information about trips with either the origin or destination located within the study area. This is a distinct disadvantage; for example, when surveying the morning or evening periods for a study area which includes a large number of workplaces and/or dwellings. The drawback can be overcome by undertaking a parking survey within the study area, concurrent with the cordon station survey. The parking zones should be carefully defined so as to relate in a meaningful way to the highway network and hence cordon stations.

### Household interview

This is the O-D survey method capable of providing the most detailed and comprehensive data, but is also generally the most costly. This is normally only justified when socio-economic information is required.

A sample of households is selected. All members of the household aged five years and over are questioned regarding all types of journeys made in one particular day. Questions are also included relating to items such as household income, car ownership, number of employed adults in household, and so on.

## Traffic variation

Traffic flows fluctuate with time: yearly, monthly, by day of week, time of day, and within the hour. Traffic flows are a function of the movements of people and as such are subject to vagaries of human nature. However, there are generally acknowledged patterns of time variation in traffic flow which are important in determining the appropriateness of traffic count data and survey periods.

The traffic flow variation by hour of day is related to the time distribution of different journey purposes. On weekdays there is typically a morning peak (say between 0800–0900 hours) of trips to work and school. This is followed by lower levels of traffic throughout the day, although perhaps with some increase exhibited around lunchtime, until school return-home trips commence. Traffic flows again peak with the concentration of work trip return journeys (say between 1700–1800 hours).

In general, weekdays have similar traffic flow patterns. It is, however, always important to be fully aware of local characteristics which may affect this, such as half-day closing or market-day. Saturday and Sunday have different traffic flow patterns from each other and from weekdays. For some developments, such as large retail schemes, it may be necessary to analyse the Saturday situation as well as the weekday.

Traffic flows are known to vary by month of year, with peak flows in the summer months and lowest flows in the winter. The months of March, April and October are considered as 'neutral' months, that is with flow levels approximating to the annual average month. In general, times of school holiday closure are generally to be avoided as counting periods, due to the effect upon travel patterns. An exception to this might be at a holiday location where analysis is required for the period of highest traffic flows; this may well coincide with the school holiday period.

The concept of annual average daily traffic (AADT) is used in highway design. As it is not practical, nor desirable, to count traffic for each day of the year and then to average the flows, it is general practice to utilize factors published by the Department of Transport to convert traffic count data to the corresponding AADT (Department of Transport, 1993). AADT (weekdays) may be considered as well as AADT (all days).

## Future traffic: design year

Historically, vehicular traffic flows have increased annually. Traffic growth is dependent upon a number of factors, but the main determinant is considered by the Department of Transport to be income, or gross domestic product (GDP), with fuel price exercising a lesser influence. The Department of Transport undertake and publish forecasts of the future levels of traffic growth: National Road Traffic Forecasts (NRTF). Growth is presently predicted throughout the time span over which the forecasts extend. That is to say, the time is not yet predicted when the traffic flows on the national highway network stabilize and exhibit little or no growth.

For the reason of anticipated traffic growth, new roads and road

improvement schemes are usually designed to be capable of accommodating traffic flows predicted for 15 years following the year of
opening. This is the approach adopted by the Department of Transport,
for motorway and trunk roads, and is usually followed by local highway
authorities responsible for the remainder of the highway network. The
objective is to provide sufficient capacity to meet predicted demand over a
significant period of the highway's design life. Otherwise, it becomes
uneconomic both in terms of delay to travellers and financial resource
allocation for improvements required.

When a proposed development is expected to generate traffic over and
above the present traffic levels, the highway authority may require that
the traffic impact of the development is predicted to be acceptable for a
future design year. This design year may be 15 years following opening of
the development (this being generally, but not always, required where the
Department of Transport is the highway authority).

However, the future design year for assessing traffic impact of the
development may well be an alternative year (earlier than 15 years) if
local conditions suggest this is appropriate (for example, programmed
highway schemes, end of local plan period).

Indeed, in some cases it is considered appropriate to assess the traffic
impact only for year of opening of the development; for example, where
the local highway network is operating at capacity (highly congested) and
'peak spreading' is occurring (peak 'hour' extends over more than one
hour due to demand in excess of capacity of highway). In such cases, the
highway cannot carry any more traffic, as exemplified by the peak
spreading already occurring. Therefore, the traffic impact of the development in the future years will not in practice lead to a worsening of the
performance of the highway links or junctions over the 'peak hour', but
can instead be expected to contribute to extension of the weekday
morning and evening peak periods (further peak spreading).

In general, it is not considered realistic to consider a future 15 year
design period as so many other factors affect the future performance of
the highway network, for example the policy of the local authority in
respect of encouraging or discouraging private car travel.

The approach generally adopted for predicting the future design year
traffic flows is to apply the Department of Transport NRTF factors. There
are two tables of factors: denoting low growth (L) and high growth (H) of
traffic. This is because the variables used to predict traffic growth are
themselves difficult to predict with precision. By using the low and high
growth factors to represent a range of traffic growth, the envelope of
predicted future year traffic flows is estimated; the lower and upper
bounds are based respectively on pessimistic and optimistic assumptions
about growth in GDP and fuel prices.

It is important to note that a major development may itself provide a
significant proportion of the traffic growth predicted for the highway

network, over the intervening period between opening of development and future design year. In these circumstances it is most likely that adoption of the low growth factor is sufficiently conservative (in ensuring that traffic growth is not underestimated). Otherwise 'double counting' of traffic growth may well occur and a highway junction scheme consequently be overdesigned.

Sometimes, it there are data available, a highway authority may adopt site-specific or local traffic growth factors which differ from the Department of Transport NRTF factors. If this is the case, these factors should be adopted for the traffic impact study, unless there are good and justifiable reasons for not doing so.

## Development analysis

The situations which typically require analysing, in respect of the traffic impact of a development upon the highway network, are:

- existing:     no development
- existing:     *with* development
- design year:  no development
- design year:  *with* development.

The objective is to assess the difference in operational performance of the highway network which is attributable to the proposed development, and to establish whether this is acceptable. This analysis identifies any highway improvement works which may be required and, where any such works are included as part of the development proposal, the 'with development' analysis models the improved highway network. Similarly, where highway improvement works are firmly programmed by the highway authority, the analysis should also consider the situation with these works complete.

## Presentation of data

The traffic data available following surveys and predictions usually requires presentation in a form which is easy and convenient to interpret. This may be in the form of tables and/or diagrams.

### Traffic counts

Traffic count data at junctions can be conveniently presented on turning count diagrams. It is important to ensure that all relevant data are included on the diagram, so that reference to the source data is not required for interpretation purposes. Items which should be included on the diagram are:

- road names
- north point
- date of survey (and day of week if relevant)
- time periods of flow data included on diagram
- location title
- units of flow presented (e.g. vehicles, passenger car units (pcu), percentage HGV and/or other classification percentages as required).

A series of junctions (and/or highway links) may be presented together on a single drawing if this is convenient.

Alternatively, traffic count data can be presented in tabular form. This is largely a matter of personal preference. However, the tabular form of presentation does not as readily lend itself to presentation of a series of junction counts so that flows at adjacent junctions can be conveniently compared.

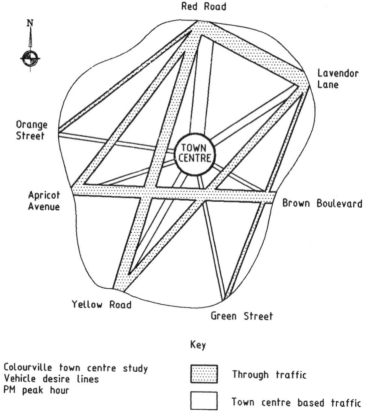

**Fig. 5.2**  Desire line diagram.

Predicted traffic data at junctions (and/or highway links) can be presented in the same manner as outlined above. The diagram should show clearly the prediction which is represented, for example 'design year 2010 L' (refer to the section 'Future traffic: design year'; earlier in this chapter), source of the base data, and the means of estimating the future year flow (value and source of factor for predicting future flows).

### Origin-destination data

The trip matrix deriving from an O-D survey can be conveniently presented in tabular form. This is particularly useful for the purposes of analysis.

A desire line diagram can provide a convenient representation of the O-D movements across the study area. This is useful when the requirement is to achieve a fairly quick and general comprehension of the predominant desire manoeuvres relative to the study area (see Figure 5.2). The width of the presented 'desire line' is proportional to the traffic flow.

## Checklist

### Traffic generation
- Identify proposed development use (and size).
- Establish time period(s) required for analysis of traffic impact.
- Estimate traffic generation for proposed development.
- Estimate or survey traffic generation for existing, recent or valid site use (pre-development).
- Estimate net additional generated traffic due to development proposal changes for the site: 'development generated' minus 'existing site generated'.
- Estimate net additional generated traffic on highway network: Estimate from above and also take account of likelihood that some of the development generated traffic may be existing traffic on network (e.g. pass-by trips).

### Distribution of generated traffic
- Estimate the likely distribution onto the highway network of development generated traffic, defining methodology adopted.
- If more than one distribution scenario appears reasonable, consider defining a distribution 'envelope' for analysis purposes, (bounded by the two scenarios envisaged possible).

### Existing traffic
- Define location(s) for which traffic count data are required.

- Establish time period(s) required for analysis (as for generated traffic, above).
- Establish whether suitable traffic count data are available from highway authority: if so, acquire.
- Undertake traffic count surveys for locations where data are not otherwise available.
- Present data in suitable manner, e.g. turning count diagram.

### Origin-destination data

- Expensive to obtain and analyse (compared with traffic count data).
- Be sure that the level of information available from an O-D study is in fact required/justified for the purposes of the project being considered.
- If required, decide on type of O-D survey technique to be adopted; in general registration number may be most convenient (if resulting level of information is adequate for study needs).
- Note: if O-D information is held by others, pursue possibility of acquiring this data and assess suitability and acceptability.

### Future traffic

- Define year of opening of development, for analysis purposes.
- Define other future design year for purpose of study analysis (if appropriate).
- Estimate future design year traffic flows, by factoring existing count data with Department of Transport NRTF factors (or local factors if applicable).
- Present design year traffic flow data in suitable manner.

### Development analysis

Usually requires analysis of the following:

Existing year    *no* development and *with* development
Design year    *no* development and *with* development

## References

Department of Transport (1981) TA11/81, *Traffic Surveys by Roadside Interview*, Department of Transport, London.

Department of Transport (1993) *Traffic Appraisal Manual* (TAM), Department of Transport, London.

# Chapter 6
# Highway Link Design

## General

Much of the consideration of traffic impact of developments relates to junction performance. However, there is often a need to consider the capacity and geometry of the length(s) of highway between junctions; the word 'link' is the technical term used to describe the length of road between junctions. Each highway link has a vehicular capacity which should not be exceeded if the road is to operate to acceptable standards, without undue delay to vehicles.

The required design geometry of the highway link is dependent upon the speeds at which vehicles will travel. Interests of highway safety are paramount. The geometric design parameters of horizontal alignment (bends, straights) and vertical alignment (gradients, crests, sags) must be appropriate to the use for which the road is intended.

Over the years the advice of the Department of Transport has modified as regards the desirable philosophy in respect of horizontal alignment. At one time it was considered that straight road alignments were generally the most safe and beneficial option. Subsequently, opinion has shifted more toward the view that introduction of horizontal curvature can be beneficial, if appropriately designed and employed. An example of this is the introduction of bends in the highway to reduce speeds in a residential area, in the interests of highway safety. There is also the difficulty that long straight stretches of highway may encourage undesirably high speeds whilst also contributing to loss of concentration due to monotony.

## Design speed

In general, drivers travel at speeds they judge to be comfortably achievable in relation to the prevailing conditions and road layout. The former includes: volume of traffic on the road, weather, and lighting conditions, all of which vary over time. The road geometry is, however, constant and can be determined by the highway authority.

Road geometry is designed to be suitable for the traffic expected to use it. The speeds anticipated on a road are the basis for deciding the appropriate road alignment. Therefore, at the design stage the design speed of the highway link must be selected. This design speed is then used to determine the physical characteristics required of the highway link.

### Factors affecting design speed

An understanding of the factors which affect the driver selected speed on a highway assists in assessing whether a proposed new road, or proposed changes to an existing highway link, are likely to be acceptable in terms of highway safety.

Speeds vary according to the perception of constraint imparted to the driver by the road layout. This constraint may be measured by three factors:

(1) Alignment constraint, $A_C$ – measures the degree of constraint imparted by the alignment, and is generally a measure of 'bendiness';
(2) Layout constraint, $L_C$ – measures the degree of constraint related to the road cross section, verge width and frequency of junctions and accesses. Table 6.1 gives values of $L_C$;
(3) Mandatory speed limits – can restrict vehicle speeds below those which might be judged by the driver to be comfortably achievable.

### Selection of design speed

The Department of Transport recommended design speed selection procedures (Department of Transport, 1993) for the following situations are:

- new rural roads – Fig. 6.1;
- existing rural road improvements – Fig. 6.1;
- urban roads – based on anticipated mandatory speed limits, with a small margin incorporated for vehicles travelling over the speed limit, as Table 6.2.

However, whilst this is commonly adopted practice for the geometric design of new works and major improvements, minor scheme design can better be based on the use of the measured 85th percentile speed of vehicles on the approach to the improvement section (see below for definition of 85th percentile speed). This is particularly relevant in respect of the highway works associated with many developments.

**Table 6.1** Layout constraint $L_C$ kph.

| Road type | S2 | | | | WS2 | | D2AP | | D3AP | D2M | D3M |
|---|---|---|---|---|---|---|---|---|---|---|---|
| Carriageway width (excluding metre strips) | 6 m | | 7.3 m | | 10 m | | Dual 7.3 m | | Dual 11 m | Dual 7.3 m and hard shoulder | Dual 11 m and hard shoulder |
| Degree of access and junctions | H | M | M | L | M | L | M | L | L | L | L |
| Standard verge width | 29 | 26 | 23 | 21 | 19 | 17 | 10 | 9 | 6 | 4 | 0 |
| 1.5 m Verge | 31 | 28 | 25 | 23 | | | | | | | |
| 0.5 m Verge | 33 | 30 | | | | | | | | | |

*Key*
S2   = Single two-lane carriageway
WS2  = Wide single two-lane carriageway
D2AP = Dual two-lane all purpose carriageway
D3AP = Dual three-lane all purpose carriageway
D2M  = Dual two-lane motorway
D3M  = Dual three-lane motorway.

*Notes*  Density of access and junctions is obtained by summing, for both sides of the road the total number of junctions, laybys and commercial accesses per km.

| | | |
|---|---|---|
| L = low access, | numbering | 2 to 5 per km |
| M = medium access, | numbering | 6 to 8 per km |
| H = high access, | numbering | 9 to 12 per km. |

*Source*  Department of Transport Departmental Standard TD 9/93, Highway Link Design.

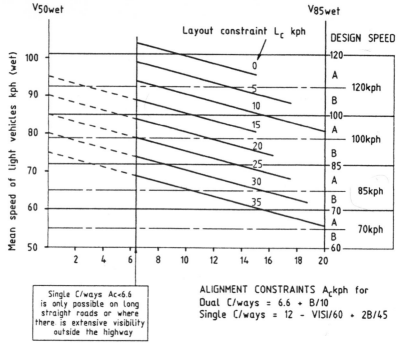

*Source:* Department of Transport Departmental Standard TD 9/93, Highway Link Design.

**Fig. 6.1** Design speed selection.

**Table 6.2** Design speed for urban roads based on mandatory speed limits envisaged.

| Speed limit | | Design speed kph |
|---|---|---|
| mph | kph | |
| 30 | 48 | 60B |
| 40 | 64 | 70A |
| 50 | 80 | 85A |
| 60 | 96 | 100A |

*Notes* The minimum design speed for a primary distributor shall be 70A kph.

*Source* Department of Transport Departmental Standard TD 9/93, Highway Link Design.

A development scheme may include proposals for one or more of the following:

- improvements to the alignment of an existing highway (e.g. improvement of bends, short diversions),
- improvements to an existing major/minor junction or access,

- introduction of a new major/minor junction or access on an existing highway.

In these cases, the 85th percentile wet weather journey speed of vehicles should be used as the design speed (see below).

### 85th percentile speed

The 85th percentile speed is the speed below which 85% of vehicles travel, in free flow conditions. Adopting the 85th percentile speed as the design speed (to determine road geometry) avoids the uneconomic circumstance of designing for the fastest driver, (which in any case might only serve to encourage undesirably high speeds); and an acceptable balance is achieved, between providing geometry which is safe for drivers, and the resultant cost of construction.

### Speed measurement

For existing highways the 85th percentile of speeds can be measured; (this should be done in the manner set out by the Department of Transport). Whilst the Department of Transport recommend that the 85th percentile wet weather journey speed is selected as the design speed for minor schemes (see 'Selection of design speed', page 44), this can be assessed without the need to undertake surveys in the wet. Nor is it necessary to undertake journey speed measurements; (these being what they sound like: speeds measured over a journey length, and concomitantly more onerous and costly to obtain than spot speeds).

Spot speed is the speed of a vehicle as it passes a specific point in the roadway, and can be measured using a radar speedmeter. The larger the sample of vehicle speeds measured, the better, in terms of reliability and representativeness of the measured vehicle speeds. The Department of Transport suggest that a sample of 200 vehicles would normally give an estimate of the 85th percentile speed for that period to within $\pm 3\%$, at the 95% confidence level. Details of the recommended survey procedure are given in the reference Department of Transport (1981).

The Department of Transport suggest that correction factors for converting dry weather spot speeds to wet weather journey speeds are:

All purpose dual carriageways    deduct 8 km/h
All purpose single carriageways    deduct 4 km/h.

In general, speeds correspond to a normal distribution curve (albeit slightly skewed). One of the properties of a normal distribution is that the 85th percentile is 1.037 standard deviations above the mean. Thus, in general the 85th percentile speed can be estimated as being one standard deviation above the measured mean speed. Indeed, if the total sample of speeds is less than 200, this is the only method recommended by the Department of Transport for estimating the 85th percentile speed.

### Existing roads: geometric standards

It is important to note that, when assessing the acceptability of the geometry of an existing highway, it is the design standards relating to the actual (occurring) 85th percentile speed which are relevant. For example, if a highway has a speed limit of 40 mph but it is considered (and verified by suitable speed survey) that the *actual* 85th percentile speed is greater than 40 mph, then the required geometry is assessed in relation to the higher *observed* 'design speed'. It should always be remembered that the underlying reasons for the standards of geometry required are the interests of highway safety.

## Geometric design parameters

Table 6.3 summarizes the values recommended by the Department of Transport for the geometric design parameters of a highway link. The design parameters included are:

Visibility     stopping sight distance (SSD)
               full overtaking sight distance (FOSD)
Alignment      horizontal curvature
               vertical curvature

all being relevant in respect of safe operation of the highway.

These parameters are all design speed related. Table 6.3 shows Desirable Minimum values (Absolute Minimum for sag curves only) and values for certain design speed steps below Desirable Minimum. The Department of Transport recommends that designers should normally aim to achieve at least Desirable Minimum values for stopping sight distance, horizontal curvature and vertical crest curvature, whilst for sag curves the aim should be to achieve at least Absolute Minimum values.

### Relaxations

Where cost and/or environmental savings are significant, relaxations may safely be made to values a given number of design steps below the Desirable Minimum; this is termed a relaxation.

The limit for relaxations varies by road type (motorway or all-purpose) and whether the design speed is band A or band B. Details of permitted relaxations for specific geometric design parameters are as follows:

(1) Relaxations should only be applied to SSD, horizontal curvature, vertical curvature and superelevation.
(2) Values for SSD, horizontal curvature and vertical curvature shall not be less than the value for 50 kph design speed in Table 6.3.
(3) Relaxations for SSD and vertical curvature for crest and sag curves are *not* permitted on the immediate approaches to junctions.

**Table 6.3** Geometry for visibility and alignment.

| Design speed (kph) | 120 | 100 | 85 | 70 | 60 | 50 | $V^2/R$ |
|---|---|---|---|---|---|---|---|
| **Stopping sight distance (SSD) (m)** | | | | | | | |
| One step below Desirable Minimum | 295 | 215 | 160 | 120 | 90 | 70 | |
| Desirable Minimum | 215 | 160 | 120 | 90 | 70 | 50 | |
| **Horizontal curvature (m)** | | | | | | | |
| Minimum R* without elimination of adverse camber and transitions | 2880 | 2040 | 1440 | 1020 | 720 | 510 | 5 |
| Minimum R* with superelevation of 2.5% | 20400 | 1440 | 1020 | 720 | 510 | 360 | 7.07 |
| Minimum R* with superelevation of 3.5% | 1440 | 1020 | 720 | 510 | 360 | 255 | 10 |
| Desirable Minimum R, superelevation 5% | 1020 | 720 | 510 | 360 | 255 | 180 | 14.14 |
| One step below Desirable Minimum R, superelevation 7% | 720 | 510 | 360 | 255 | 180 | 127 | 20 |
| Two steps below Desirable Minimum R, superelevation 7% | 510 | 360 | 255 | 180 | 127 | 90 | 28.28 |
| **Vertical curvature** | | | | | | | |
| Desirable Minimum *Crest K value | 182 | 100 | 55 | 30 | 17 | 10 | |
| One step below Desirable Minimum Crest K value | 100 | 55 | 30 | 17 | 10 | 6.5 | |
| Absolute minimum sag K value | 37 | 26 | 20 | 20 | 13 | 9 | |
| **Overtaking sight distance (m)** | | | | | | | |
| FOSD overtaking Crest K value | * | 400 | 285 | 200 | 142 | 100 | |

* Not recommended for use in the design of single carriageways.

*Source* Department of Transport Departmental Standard TD 9/93, Highway Link Design.

(4) Number of design speed steps below the Desirable Minimum for which relaxations are normally permitted, subject to (1)–(3) above, are:

| Road type | Design speed band | Number of design speed steps permitted below the Desirable Minimum | | |
|---|---|---|---|---|
| | | SSD | Horizontal curvature | Crest curves |
| Motorway | A | 1 | 2 | 1 |
| | B | 2 | 3 | 2 |
| All-purpose | A | 2 | 3 | 2 |
| | B | 3 | 4 | 3 |

(5) For sag curves the number of design speed steps permitted below the Absolute Minimum are normally:

| Road type | Design speed band | Number of design speed steps permitted below the Absolute Minimum |
|---|---|---|
| Motorway | | none |
| All-purpose | all others | 1 |
| All-purpose | 50B, 60B, 70B | 2 |

(6) Guidance for extending or reducing scope for relaxations of (4) and (5) above is provided by the Department of Transport (1981).

## Stopping sight distance (SSD)

This is the theoretical sight distance a driver needs to safely stop a vehicle when confronted by an unexpected obstruction or hazard in the carriageway. The SSD has two elements, being:

- perception-reaction distance – distance travelled from the time the driver sees the hazard to the time it is realized that the vehicle must be halted;
- braking distance – distance travelled during time from commencement of deceleration to stopping of the vehicle.

Both the perception-reaction distance and the braking distance can only be estimated; in practice these will not be constant for all vehicles under all conditions. The perception-reaction time can vary significantly between drivers and also for the same driver at different times (being affected by tiredness, age and other factors). The actual braking distance depends upon the vehicle performance and road condition, and also the speed at which the driver is actually travelling (the estimated braking distance assumes the vehicle is travelling at the design speed of the highway and that the vehicle is halted just short of the observed hazard).

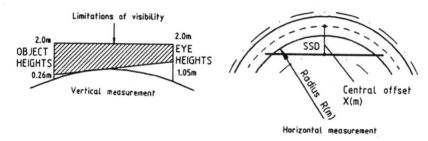

*Source:* Department of Transport Departmental Standard TD 9/93, Highway Link Design.

**Fig. 6.2** Measurement of SSD.

Thus estimates of stopping sight distance are derived using variable estimates which can not be accurate for all cases.

The forward visibility required for safe stopping is between the driver's eye and the obstruction. The SSD should be measured as shown in Fig. 6.2. This takes account of the following:

- 95% of drivers of private vehicles have eye heights of at least 1.05 m above the road surface,
- 2.0 m is taken as the upper limit of eye height, to represent drivers of large or high vehicles,
- height of obstruction is assumed to be between 0.26 m (low) and 2.0 m (high).

Forward visibility should be available in both the horizontal and vertical planes, between any two points in the centre of the lane nearest the inside of the curve (for each carriageway in the case of dual carriageways).

## Full overtaking sight distance (FOSD)

On single carriageway roads, an overtaking vehicle must generally utilize the opposing traffic lane. For safe overtaking the sight distance must be adequate to ensure completion of the manoeuvre without conflict with an opposing oncoming vehicle.

The elements involved in an overtaking manoeuvre are:

- *perception-reaction distance* – distance travelled by the vehicle while the driver decides whether or not to overtake,
- *overtaking distance* – distance travelled while the vehicle undertakes the overtaking manoeuvre,
- *closing distance* – distance travelled by oncoming vehicle while the overtaking manoeuvre is undertaken,
- *safety distance* – separation distance needed between the oncoming vehicle and the overtaking vehicle at the instant the latter returns to its own lane.

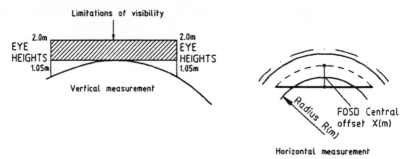

Source:    Department of Transport Departmental Standard TD 9/93, Highway Link Design.

**Fig. 6.3**    Measurement of FOSD.

The time taken to undertake the complete sequence outlined above is dependent upon the relative speeds of the vehicles involved. As a guide, some 85% of overtaking manoeuvres take less than 10 seconds.

The FOSD values in Table 6.3 are calculated based on the design speed of the road. In rural locations it may be feasible to provide the FOSD, although this can normally only be economically provided where the topography is conducive to providing a flat and relatively straight road alignment.

In urban locations, however, it is rarely practicable to provide FOSD, for reasons of cost (including factors such as land ownership and use). In any case, in an urban location the nature and control of the single carriageway highway network often inhibits overtaking.

FOSD should be available between points 1.05 m and 2.0 m above the centre of the carriageway, as shown on Fig. 6.3, and should be checked in both the horizontal and vertical planes.

## Horizontal alignment

Based on the design speed of the road, the values for horizontal curvature presented in Table 6.3, (for different superelevations), are recommended by the Department of Transport. These are also widely adopted by local highway authorities.

### Superelevation

Friction is generated between the wheels of a moving vehicle and the carriageway surface. A vehicle is subject to centrifugal force as it travels round a bend. If the friction between vehicle and road surface is not in itself sufficient to offset the centrifugal force generated, the vehicle may slide, or in the extreme, overturn. Thus superelevation (also known as camber or crossfall) is provided on a bend to prevent this occurring.

Table 6.3 lists recommended values of horizontal curvature for superelevations of 2.5%, 3.5%, 5% and 7%. When $V^2/R$ is greater than 7, the required superelevation can be calculated from:

$$S = \frac{V^2}{2.828\,R} \qquad (6.1)$$

where  S = superelevation,               %
        V = velocity, i.e. design speed,   kph
        R = radius of curve,               m.

On horizontal curves, adverse camber should be replaced by favourable crossfall of 2.5%, when $V^2/R$ is between 5 and 7. In rural areas, maximum superelevation of 70% is recommended. In urban areas with at-grade (single level) junctions and side accesses, it is recommended that superelevation is restricted to 5% maximum.

### Transition curves

When superelevation is applied, or adverse camber is removed, this should be achieved progressively. There must be some transition from the state of 'no superelevation' to that of 'full superelevation'; this occurs over the length of a 'transition curve'.

The transition curve is defined by the mathematical formula:

$$L = \frac{V^3}{46.7\,q\,R} \qquad (6.2)$$

where  L = length of transition curve,            m
        V = design speed,                     kph
        q = rate of increase of radial acceleration,   $m/sec^3$
        R = radius of curve,                  m.

Notes:
(1) q should normally not exceed $0.3\ m/sec^3$. However, in urban areas it may commonly be necessary to accept q of $0.6\ m/sec^3$, (or even higher in especially difficult locations).
(2) The calculated transition length L (appropriate to the design speed) may be insufficient to accommodate the superelevation turnover, and in such cases should be increased as necessary to suit the superelevation design.

## Vertical alignment

The natural effect of a vertical gradient is to reduce vehicle speeds on ascent and to increase speed on the descent. This is particularly applicable to heavy commercial vehicles. The disbenefits of steep vertical gradients include disruption to vehicle flow and increase in safety hazard.

### Gradient

The recommended desirable maximum gradients are presented in Table

**Table 6.4**   Vertical gradients: recommendations of Department of Transport.

| Road type | Desirable maximum gradient % |
|---|---|
| Motorway | 3 |
| All purpose dual carriageway | 4 |
| All purpose single carriageway | 5 |

6.4. Steeper gradients may be justified in areas of hilly topography, taking account of cost and environmental factors. However, the higher the traffic flows, the greater the consequences to traffic of accepting the steeper gradient. As gradients become progressively steeper, so there is a decrease in safety. The Department of Transport consider a gradient in excess of 8% to be a departure from standards. The road design must provide suitable means of surface water drainage. With kerbed roads a minimum of 0.5% vertical gradient enables effective drainage. However, in flatter areas this can be achieved by suitable rise and fall of kerbside drainage channels.

## Vertical curves

Vertical curves are required at all changes in gradient. Visibility requirements must always be considered, in the interests of highway safety.

Vertical curves are designed to be parabolic (as this provides a constant rate of curvature). A vertical curve can be a 'crest' or 'sag' curve. The length of curve is calculated from:

$$L = KA \qquad\qquad (6.3)$$

where   L = curve length,                    m
        K = design speed related coefficient,   (from Table 6.3)
        A = algebraic difference in grades,    %

*Example:*
Grade change from       +2.5% to −3%
                        A = 5.5
Design speed            85 kph
From Table 6.3          one step below Desirable Minimum K value for crest curve is 30

Thus,   $L = 30 \times 5.5 = 165$ m (for one step below Desirable Minimum)

Desirable Minimum would similarly be

$L = 55 \times 5.5 = 302.5$ m.

For crest curves, the Desirable Minimum values are based on visibility criteria.

## Coordination of horizontal and vertical alignments

It is desirable to coordinate horizontal and vertical alignments, in the interests of highway safety (to avoid optical illusions which create a safety hazard). This is a matter of detail design. One way of achieving this is to ensure that all points where horizontal and vertical changes occur coincide with each other.

## Checklist

### Design speed of road
- Determinant factor of required highway geometry (for highway safety).
- Corresponds to observed or predicted 85th percentile speed.
- Determined as follows:
  Rural roads:    Fig. 6.1
  Urban roads:    Table 6.2
  Measured 85th percentile speed may be better alternative (for existing roads).

### Visibility
- Stopping sight distance (SSD): Table 6.3
- Full overtaking sight distance (FOSD): Table 6.3; rarely practicable to provide FOSD in urban locations.

### Horizontal alignment
- Radius of curve: Table 6.3.
- Superelevation: generally maximum 5% urban areas, maximum 7% rural areas.
- Transition curve: to apply superelevation.

### Vertical alignment
- Gradient: maximum recommended as Table 6.4.
- Length of vertical curve: calculate from $L = KA$. (K, from Table 6.3, is design speed dependent; A is grade change.)

## References

Department of Transport (1981) TA 22/81, *Vehicle Speed Measurement on All-Purpose Roads*, Department of Transport, London.
Department of Transport (1993) TD9/93, *Highway Link Design, and Amendment No. 1*, Department of Transport, London.

# Chapter 7
# Priority Junctions

## General

The simplest form of controlled junction design is the major and minor priority arrangement, where the major road traffic has priority over that on the minor road. Control can be either by 'give way' or 'stop' road markings and signs. Priority should be given to the road carrying the heaviest volume of traffic.

Generally, for the same major and minor road traffic flows, a priority control junction will have an increased likelihood of accident occurrence, compared with the alternative junction controls of roundabout (Chapter 8) or traffic signals (Chapter 9).

The major manoeuvres which can take place at a junction are illustrated in Fig. 7.1.

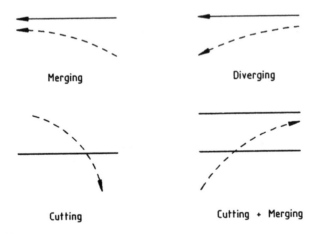

**Fig. 7.1** Junction manoeuvres.

## At-grade intersections

The term 'at-grade' refers to junctions with intersecting roads meeting at a common level. The general forms of at-grade junction layout which

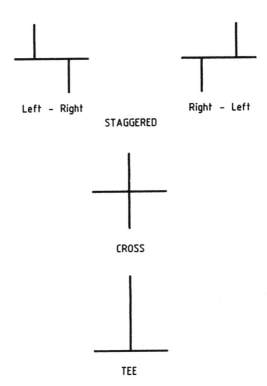

**Fig. 7.2** At-grade junction layouts.

occur are illustrated on Fig. 7.2. The three main forms of priority junction are:

- T-junction
- staggered junction
- crossroads.

Of these, a T-junction is the preferred layout. Crossroads are generally to be avoided if at all possible (for junctions operating under priority control), for reasons of highway safety.

If a crossing manoeuvre is required (at a junction operating under priority control), a stagger double T-junction layout should be considered as an alternative to a crossroads arrangement. For stagger junctions, a right-left stagger is preferred (minor road traffic crossing major road first turns right out of the minor road, proceeds along the major road and then turns left; Fig. 7.2), both in terms of traffic flow and safety. (This layout reduces the number of vehicles turning right off the major road. Additionally, with the alternative of a left-right stagger, vehicles waiting to turn right, to either side off the major road, share the same reservoir length between side roads, with the associated potential for vehicular conflict. The right-left stagger avoids this, as those vehicles turning right off the major road wait outside the stagger length between the two T-junctions.)

# Channelization

Suitable road markings and traffic islands should be provided to separate the manoeuvres illustrated on Fig. 7.1. This improves the safety of the junction, whilst increasing the capacity.

Channelization is the application of measures designed to separate two or more traffic streams, each stream being confined to a single roadway channel. The main reasons for channelization are:

- Diminish the number of possible conflicts by reducing possible carriageway area of conflict.
- Control angle of vehicle conflict.
- Reduce speed of traffic entering a junction.
- Provide protection for vehicles leaving or crossing the main traffic stream.
- Regulate traffic movement by island location and shape.
- Provide refuge for pedestrians.

In many situations channelization realizes more than one of the aims outlined above. In all cases, if well designed and appropriate channelization measures are introduced, improvement is achieved in terms of highway safety.

# Types of major/minor junction

## *Single carriageways*

There are three basic categories of layout for major/minor priority junctions on single carriageway roads: simple, ghost island and single lane dualling. The main features of these are summarized in Table 7.1.

With ghost island and single lane dualling layouts, the island defines a central line: the *right-turning lane*. This serves the purposes of:

- diverging lane and waiting space for major road right-turning vehicles,
- avoiding restricting capacity for straight-ahead major road traffic (due to impedance by waiting major road right-turn vehicles),
- waiting space for minor road vehicles undertaking a 'cut and merge' manoeuvre (Fig. 7.1).

**Table 7.1** Types of major/minor junction: Single carriageways.

| Junction type | Major road islands | Use |
|---|---|---|
| Simple | No ghost or physical islands | • *New* rural accesses and junctions; maximum 300 two-way AADT on minor road |
| | | • *Existing rural* and at *urban* accesses and junctions; maximum 500 two-way AADT on minor road |
| Ghost island | Painted hatched island in middle of major road | Busy accesses and junctions where flows exceed 'simple' flows |
| Single lane dualling | Physical island in middle of major road | Busy junctions widely spaced on rural roads; design speed at least 35 kph |

*Note* AADT is 'annual average daily traffic' (see Chapter 5).

### Dual carriageways

For dual carriageway roads, local widening of the central reservation should be employed to provide the diverging and waiting space for right-turning traffic (the *right-turning lane*). This is comparable to the single lane dualling situation, where a physical island is introduced onto the major road carriageway.

### Channelizing islands in minor road

It is recommended that channelizing islands are provided in the minor road approaches for all but the most lightly trafficked junctions. In practical terms this achieves the following:

- provides guidance to long vehicles when undertaking turning manoeuvres,
- protects vehicles waiting to turn right from the major road,
- warns drivers on the minor road that there is a junction ahead,
- helps pedestrians crossing the minor road.

These are all positive advantages in terms of highway safety.

## Recommended junction layouts

The Department of Transport publish recommended layouts for major/minor junctions, for various combinations of major road carriageway

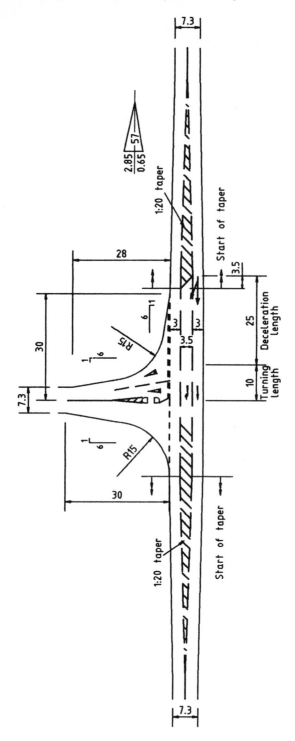

*Notes*
(1) Widening on junction side only.
(2) All dimensions in metres.

*Source*   Department of Transport Departmental Advice Note TA 20/84, Junctions and Accesses: the layout of major/minor junctions.

**Fig. 7.3**   Typical T-junction layout 50/60 kph design speed.

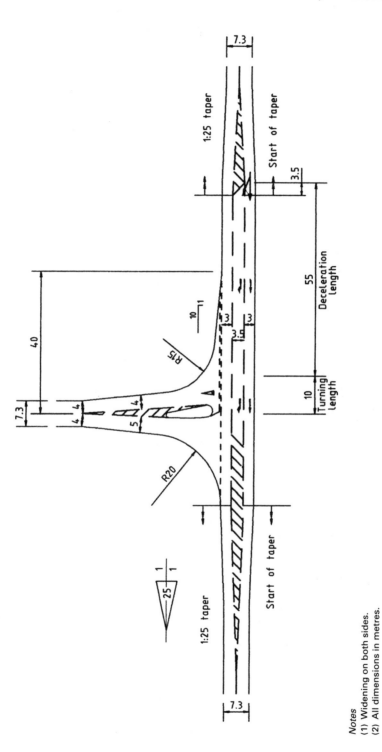

*Source* Department of Transport Departmental Advice Note TA 20/84, Junctions and Accesses: the layout of major/minor junctions.

**Fig. 7.4** Typical T-junction layout 85A kph design speed.

width and traffic speed (Department of Transport, 1984). These provide a good starting point for design of a major/minor junction layout. It must always be remembered, however, that common sense should be employed when considering site-specific situations. Rigid adherence to guidelines should not be permitted to preclude a measured consideration of the justification for providing a given type of layout; there may sometimes be a case for modifications tailored to suit specific circumstances, most commonly in existing situations where scope for improvement is limited. In all cases, considerations of highway safety are of paramount importance, but must be appraised in the context of likely occurrence of conditions.

Figures 7.3 and 7.4 are examples of Department of Transport recommended junction layouts for single carriageway T-junctions. A total of 29 examples of junction layouts are presented by the Department of Transport (Department of Transport, 1984), to provide guidance to the designer for the types of junction most frequently encountered in practice.

### Right-turning lanes

A right-turning lane arrangement (at ghost island, single lane dualling and dual carriageway junctions) has the following components: offside diverging lane, island, through lanes. The recommended dimensions are presented in Table 7.2.

The Department of Transport recommend that the central islands (be they ghost or physical islands) should normally be developed symmetrically about the centre line of the major road to their maximum width, at the tapers shown in Table 7.5 (and see Fig. 7.6). However, sometimes islands should be introduced asymmetrically to suit the circumstances, such as on sharp curves. Similarly, it may be advantageous to introduce islands asymmetrically in consideration of cost and/or land availability, and this is quite permissible. Examples of such situations are: the avoidance of the plant of statutory undertakers and the need to avoid land in third party ownership.

### Nearside diverging lane (deceleration lane)

Nearside diverging lanes permit traffic turning left off the major road to slow down and leave the major road without impeding following through traffic, being of benefit in both capacity and highway safety terms. Table 7.6 summarizes the conditions for use and recommended geometry.

### Merging lane (acceleration lane)

Merging lanes allow left-turning minor road traffic to accelerate before joining the major road traffic. The decrease in differential between speeds

**Table 7.2** Offside diverging lanes: recommended dimensions.

| Junction type | Offside diverging lane | | | Island | | Through lanes |
| --- | --- | --- | --- | --- | --- | --- |
| | Lane[2] length | Lane width | Taper/splay | Desirable width | Absolute minimum width | |
| Ghost | Table 7.3 + 10m | As island width | Introduce[3] lane by 45° splay (Fig. 7.5) | 3.5[4] | 3.0[5] | 3.0–3.65[6] |
| Single Lane[1] Dualling | Table 7.3 + 10m | 3.5 | Direct Taper[8] (Fig. 7.7 and Table 7.4) | 10.0[7] | Not specified | 4.0[6] |
| Dual[1] Carriageway | Table 7.3 + 10m | 3.5 | | | | Maintain lane widths remote from junction |

*Notes:*
(1) Physical island.
(2) Lane length depends on major road design speed (Chapter 6) and gradient.
L = deceleration length + turning length.
Deceleration length in Table 7.3.
Turning length *always* 10 m.
(3) Splay length is part of the deceleration length. The exception to the rule is at a left-right stagger.
(4) At urban and suburban junctions, a width of 5 m may be advantageous, where a significant occurrence of large (long) turning vehicles is expected. This is to provide additional shelter to minor road vehicles undertaking the 'cut and merge' manoeuvre.
(5) Where space is limited, a reduced width may be unavoidable. Where the Department of Transport is the highway authority, reductions below 3 m must be specially authorized, with the width never permitted to be less than 2.5 m.
(6) Exclusive of hardstrips.
(7) Including central reserve hardstrips.
(8) Taper length (Table 7.4) is included as part of the required deceleration length (Table 7.3).

**Table 7.3**   Offside diverging lane: deceleration length (m).

| Design[1] speed (kph) | Ghost island and single lane dualling | | | Dual carriageway | | |
|---|---|---|---|---|---|---|
| | Up or down[2] | Up[2] | Down[2] | Up or down[2] | Up[2] | Down[2] |
| | 0–4% | >4% | >4% | 0–4% | 0–4% | >4% |
| 120A | 110 | 80 | 110 | 110 | 80 | 150 |
| 100A | 80 | 55 | 80 | 80 | 55 | 110 |
| 85A | 55 | 40 | 55 | 55 | 40 | 80 |
| 70A | 40 | 25 | 40 | 40 | 25 | 55 |
| 60A | 25 | 25 | 25 | 25 | 25 | 40 |
| 50A | 25 | 25 | 25 | 25 | 25 | 25 |

*Notes*
(1) Design speed of major road (see Chapter 6).
(2) Gradient (up or down) is the average over the 150 m length before the minor road.

For Category B design speeds (see Chapter 6), the lower value should be used (in the up or down mode as appropriate), irrespective of gradient.

**Table 7.4**   Taper length.

| Design speed (m) | L (m) |
|---|---|
| 120 | 30 |
| 100 | 25 |
| 85 | 15 |
| 70 | 15 |
| 60 | 5 |
| 50 | 5 |

*Source*   Department of Transport Departmental Advice Note TA 20/84, Junctions and Accesses: the layout of major/minor junctions.

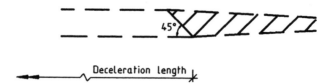

*Source*   Department of Transport Departmental Advice Note TA 20/84, Junctions and Accesses: the layout of major/minor junctions.

**Fig. 7.5**   Offside diverging lane: ghost island taper, 45° splay.

**Table 7.5** Tapers for developing central islands.

| Design speed (kph) | X (Taper at '1 in X') | |
| --- | --- | --- |
| | Ghost island and single lane dualling | Dual carriageway |
| 120 | n/a | 55 |
| 100 | 30 | 50 |
| 85 | 25 | 45 |
| 70 | 20 | 40 |
| 60 | 20 | 40 |
| 50 | 20 | 40 |

*Source* Department of Transport Departmental Advice Note TA 20/84, Junctions and Accesses: the layout of major/minor junctions.

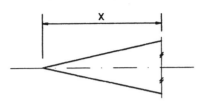

*Source* Department of Transport Departmental Advice Note TA 20/84, Junctions and Accesses: the layout of major/minor junctions.

**Fig. 7.6** Tapers at which islands are developed (see Table 7.5).

of minor road (joining) traffic and major road through traffic is beneficial in terms of increased capacity and highway safety. Table 7.6 summarizes the conditions for use and recommended geometry.

### Stagger distances

Recommended minimum stagger distances (between the centre lines of the minor roads at entry to the major road) are presented in Table 7.7.

### Traffic islands and refuges

The recommendations are:

Minimum area      4.5 m$^2$
Minimum width    1.2 m, where serving as refuge for pedestrians.

When used by pedestrians, there should be openings in the centre of the island at carriageway level, or dropped kerbs. Complementarily, dropped kerbs should be provided opposite the refuge openings.

**Table 7.6**  Use and geometry: nearside diverging lanes (deceleration lane), merging lanes (acceleration lane).

| Lane facility | Use at junctions | | | | Geometry |
|---|---|---|---|---|---|
| | Simple | Ghost | Single dualling | Dual carriageway | |
| Merging | No | No | No | Yes, where design speed* > 85 kph and minor road LT >600 AADT | Initial width   Min 3.5 m<br>Decreases at taper of:<br><br>Design speed   Taper<br>120   1 : 20<br>100   1 : 15<br>85   1 : 15 |
| Nearside diverging | No | Yes<br><br>*If* design speed > 85 kph and<br>(i) LT traffic > 600 vehicles AADT<br>or<br>(ii) HGVs > 20% and LT >450 AADT<br>or<br>Any design speed and junction is on up or down gradient > 4% and LT > 450 AADT | | | Width   3.5 m<br>Direct taper<br>Length of lane:<br>   Maximum as Table 7.3<br>   Minimum = 0.5 maximum<br>   Absolute minimum = 35 m<br><br>(Length defined from beginning of taper) |

*Note* * Design speed – see Chapter 6.

LT = left turning traffic.

**Table 7.7** Minimum stagger distances.

| Stagger | Design speed (kph) | Recommended minimum stagger distance at junction type (m) | | | |
|---|---|---|---|---|---|
| | | Simple | Ghost | Single lane dualling | Dual carriageway |
| Right/left[1,2] | All | 50 | 40 | 50 | 60 |
| Left/right[3] | All | 50 | | | |
| | 120 | | | | 130 |
| | 100 | | 100 | 100 | 100 |
| | 85 | | 75 | 75 | 75 |
| | 70 | | 60 | | 60 |
| | 60 | | 50 | | 60 |
| | 50 | | 50 | | 60 |

*Notes*
(1) Based on vehicle manoeuvre of 18 m long drawbar trailer combination.
(2) Right/left stagger is preferred.
(3) Based on sum of the two deceleration lengths (Table 7.3) lying side by side, plus the turning lengths at each end. Values in table relate to Category A design speed roads (see Chapter 6), but they can vary with Category B design speeds and with gradients (see Table 7.3).

Where no value is given for length this is because the situation does not apply.

## Visibility

Minor road traffic joins or crosses the major road traffic when there are suitable gaps in the major road traffic flow. Therefore, the emerging minor road traffic must have adequate visibility to judge the major road traffic gaps and undertake the desired turning manoeuvres with safety.

Complementarily, the straight-ahead major road traffic must have adequate forward sight distance of the minor road traffic, so as to be able to safely decelerate or stop if necessary (stopping sight distance). Similarly, traffic turning right off the major road into the minor road must have adequate forward visibility to judge gaps in the opposing major road traffic stream.

For the emerging minor road traffic the sightlines should be available

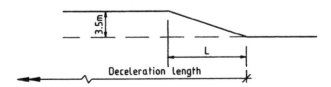

*Source* Department of Transport Departmental Advice Note TA 20/84, Junctions and Accesses: the layout of major/minor junctions.

**Fig. 7.7** Offside diverging lane: physical island direct taper.

between two points 1.05 m above the road level, and may be conveniently described by 'X' and 'Y' dimensions, measured as shown on Fig. 7.8.

The Department of Transport recommend an 'X' dimension of 9 m for new junctions and improvements to existing junctions. However, in many circumstances, for particular development uses and/or at more lightly trafficked junctions with physical constraints, a lesser 'X' dimension may be acceptable, being variously reduced to 4.5 m, 3.0 m, 2.5 m, 2.4 m or even 2.0 m. The requirements tend to vary between highway authorities and for each development the appropriate standard should be discussed with the highway authority at the early design stages, particularly if there is likely to be any difficulty in providing the 9 m 'X' dimension, or if this is not appropriate (for example, residential development).

The 'Y' distance must be such that the major road traffic has sufficient forward visibility to stop with safety, if so required, this corresponding to the stopping sight distance as set out in Table 6.3, (Chapter 6). The 'Y' dimension should be achieved in both directions. However, some highway authorities accept a reduced 'Y' to the left (measuring only to the centreline of the road) if the full distance cannot be provided. Visibility requirements depend upon the major road speed. Table 7.8 summarizes the 'Y' requirement for different vehicle speeds.

# Capacity

## General

The approach adopted for predicting capacity, and hence performance, of a priority junction is empirically based. This means that the formulae used to model the behaviour of a priority junction are derived from data of observed performance. The alternative approach, of developing a theoretically based model, is not adopted. This is because of the difficulty encountered to date in developing a theoretical model which performs satisfactorily, as the vehicle-vehicle interactions are very complex.

## Three-arm junction

A set of relationships is derived for the traffic stream capacities at a priority junction. The basic model is for a three-arm junction, which has six separate traffic streams, as indicated in Fig. 7.9. Of these, the straight-ahead major road streams (C-A and A-C) and the left-turn stream off the major road (A-B) have uninterrupted priority; thus being generally assumed to suffer no delay due to other traffic. It should be noted that with some geometric layouts the straight-ahead traffic stream C-A may suffer delay due to the right-turning C–B vehicles waiting on the major road carriageway; the optimum layout is designed to avoid such restriction to straight-ahead traffic flows. The two minor road streams (B-A and B-C)

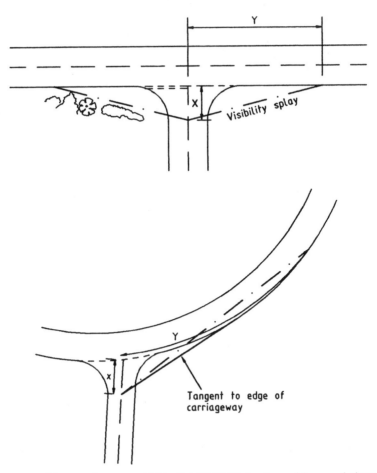

*Source* Department of Transport Departmental Advice Note TA 20/84, Junctions and Accesses: the layout of major/minor junctions.

**Fig. 7.8** Visibility splay.

must give way to the priority (controlling) streams and delay may thus be incurred; similarly for the major road right-turn stream (C-B).

The capacity of a non-priority (controlled) arm depends upon the major road flows to which the stream has to give way. The stream capacities are developed as explicit functions of the controlling major road flows and the junction geometry.

Geometric parameters in the capacity prediction formulae include:

- lane width – non-priority streams
- widths on major road carriageway, including central reserve (if applicable)
- visibility for non-priority traffic.

**Table 7.8** Visibility requirements.

| Design speed* (kph) | Y dimension (m) |
|---|---|
| 120 | 295 |
| 100 | 215 |
| 85 | 160 |
| 70 | 120 |
| 60 | 90 |
| 50 | 70 |

*Notes* * The design speed of a major road is normally the 85th percentile of actual vehicle speeds for an existing road, or the relevant design speed for a new road (see Chapter 6).

*Source* Department of Transport Departmental Advice Note TA 20/84, Junctions and Accesses: the layout of major/minor junctions.

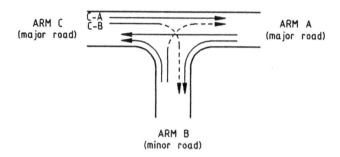

**Fig. 7.9** Priority T-junction.

### Four-arm junction

The capacity of a four-arm junction is similarly calculated as a function of controlling flows and geometric characteristics. The calculations are more complex than for three-arm junctions due to additional traffic streams.

### Accuracy

The accuracy of predicted capacity and performance reflects the accuracy of data input to the predictive model; the results can at best only have a precision the same as the information which is used within the analysis. Care should therefore be taken in estimating input data.

Where there is doubt, it may be wise to adopt conservative values for input to analysis; in this way the output may be most robust. This is especially important if there is some disagreement between interested parties in respect of the adequacy of a junction layout for specific circumstances. However, it is not in anyone's interests to be unduly conservative and thereby 'overdesign' a junction. In some cases, sensitivity testing may be usefully achieved by analysing both the perceived likely 'optimistic' and 'pessimistic' scenarios in respect of estimated input data, thereby enabling a fuller understanding of likely junction performance under critical traffic flow conditions.

The predictive capacity formulae were empirically derived using standard statistical techniques, and based on observed data for many sites. There is, therefore, uncertainty of prediction within the formulae, arising from 'within-site' variation and 'between-site' variation (of the observed data used to develop the predictive equations). The effect of within-site variation for a single site is very small (of the order of a few vehicles per hour). The main uncertainties are associated with the between-sites variation. Thus, for a typical site, the standard error of the capacity prediction is about 13%, taking account of both the 'random' variability between supposedly identical sites and the 'random' variability that may occur at a single site at different times of the day.

# Analysis methods

## *Manual*

It is not recommended that the entry flow calculation is undertaken manually. This is primarily because of the much greater time taken for calculation to achieve the comparable level of analysis compared with computation. Also, predicted queue lengths can not be manually calculated.

It should also be noted that manual calculation necessitates the application of a factor of 1.125 to the traffic flow volumes input to the predictive equations. This is to allow for short term variations in traffic flow. The Department of Transport computer program available for analysing priority junctions models the traffic flows to take account of this.

## *Measures of priority junction performance*

The measure commonly used to assess the performance of a non-priority traffic stream (at a major or minor priority junction) is referred to as the *RFC*; this is the ratio of the demand traffic flow to the capacity. The demand traffic flow is observed for existing situations in time (traffic counts: refer Chapter 5). Future year traffic flows are estimated in accordance with the procedures outlined in Chapter 5; (observed traffic flow data are factored to future design year flow estimates using the Department of Transport NRTF factors as appropriate, or other local factors as available).

Common engineering practice, (as recommended by the Department of Transport), is to consider a RFC value of 0.85 as the upper desirable value, for operation to acceptable standards of a junction approach lane.

The queue length on a non-priority lane can often be critical in operational terms; for example, if it is likely to extend back to block an adjacent junction or significant access (such as a fire station exit). This should be taken into account when assessing the acceptability of junction arrangements for anticipated traffic demands.

### Computer program: PICADY

The most widely used computer program for analysing major-minor priority junction performance is the Department of Transport's PICADY. Three-arm (T-junction) and four-arm (crossroads, right-left staggered and left-right staggered) major-minor priority junctions can be analysed. The available features include tabulation of predicted RFC values, queue lengths and delays for a defined time period. The selected time period is modelled in user-specified time segments (say, 15 minutes).

The program has a number of optional features, such as accident prediction and the facility to specify a 'queue marker' for a non-priority stream. Accident analysis is restricted to rural T-junctions or staggered junctions. If the queue marker option is stipulated, the program output reports the probability of the queue extending back to the queue marker or beyond, for each time segment of the period modelled. This probability can be converted into estimated number of days per year that the queue will reach the marker.

The program can take account of the effect of a pedestrian crossing installed close to the junction; this may reduce the vehicular capacity of the junction in two ways. Firstly, for traffic approaching the junction, the combined capacity of the crossing and junction will be lower than either the vehicular capacity of the crossing or the junction considered separately. Secondly, the crossing may restrict traffic leaving the junction, causing 'blocking back' (queuing traffic blocks the junction area).

## Practical points of design

The analysis described above relates to capacity prediction. This is an important aid in the achievement of a good priority junction design. However, in the overall design process a number of other factors, which are not explicitly included in the capacity analysis procedure, must also be taken into account. These factors include:

- standards of visibility,
- space requirements for large turning flows of heavy vehicles,
- design of ghost island and physical islands, and central reserve openings at dual carriageway sites,
- provision of deceleration and acceleration lanes,
- lighting provision,

- use of signs, road markings and road furniture
- aesthetic considerations.

The recommendations in respect of visibility, islands, deceleration and acceleration lanes (nearside diverging lanes and merging lanes respectively) are summarized in the earlier parts of this chapter.

The junction layout under consideration should be checked against the swept path requirements for large vehicles. This is to ensure that large (long) vehicles can complete manoeuvres in an acceptable manner, for example, without necessity for the swept wheel path to infringe upon the footway or onto the roadway space reserved for opposing traffic flow. This is in the interests of highway safety and to avoid unnecessary and costly damage to the highway (an example is where an inadequate corner radius results in goods vehicles regularly riding over the corner kerb and consequently damaging the footway). However, it is also important that the likely traffic demand from large (long) vehicles is considered in determining an economic design.

The corner radii to be provided at the junction may typically be in a range of perhaps 6–15 m, depending upon the level of turning demand from long vehicles. Typically, a corner radius of 10–15 m can satisfactorily accommodate long turning vehicles. However, the corner radius provided may necessarily be of a lesser dimension if land ownerships are restrictive.

A proposed junction layout should always take cognisance of land availability/ownership. Also, the location of the plant of statutory undertakers should be ascertained, to avoid proposing a junction layout which incurs unnecessarily high and/or prohibitively high costs due to relocation of plant.

## Checklist

### Forms of priority junction
- The three main forms of priority junction are: T-junction, staggered junction and crossroads.
- T-junction is the preferred layout.
- Crossroads are generally to be avoided. For crossing manoeuvres a stagger junction arrangement should be considered as the alternative to the crossroads; the right-left stagger is preferred.

### Types of major/minor junction
- Single carriageways see Table 7.1.

| Simple | No ghost or physical islands |
| Ghost island | Painted hatched island in major road. |
| Single lane dualling | Physical island in major road. |

- Dual carriageways.
Local widening of central reservation to provide 'right-turning lane'.

### Recommended junction layouts
Design features may include:

- Right-turning lane (from major road into minor road). Components are offside diverging lane, island (ghost or physical) and through lanes.
- Channelizing islands in the minor road approaches (recommended).
- Nearside diverging lane (deceleration lane).
- Merging lane (acceleration lane).

### Visibility
- Visibility splay required for safety (of emerging minor road traffic and major road right-turning traffic).
- See Table 7.8.

### Capacity
- Non-priority traffic streams (i.e. give-way) are the minor road lanes and the major road right-turn. These capacities are defined, by empirically derived formulae, as functions of the controlling major road flows and the junction geometry.
- The geometric parameters in the capacity prediction formulae include:
  ○ lane width – non-priority streams,
  ○ widths on major road carriageway, including central reserve (if applicable),
  ○ visibility for non-priority traffic.
- PICADY – Department of Transport computer program to analyse performance of major/minor priority junctions.

### Practical design
- Proposed solution should take account of land ownerships.
- Location of the plant of statutory undertakers should be ascertained.

# References

Department of Transport (1984) TA 20/84, *Junctions and Accesses: the layout of major/minor junctions*, Department of Transport, London.

# Chapter 8
# Roundabouts

## History

### Priority

Prior to 1966, the priority of one traffic stream over another was not defined at roundabouts. Hence, the early designs suffered from a tendency to 'lock' under heavy traffic. To try and reduce the probability of this occurring, long lengths of circulating carriageway, known as 'weaving sections', were increasingly used between successive entries. This often resulted in very large designs.

The offside priority rule was introduced in November 1966 (give-way to vehicles from the right), and the phenomenon of locking disappeared. Subsequently, much smaller designs were developed, giving greater efficiency of land use. Such arrangements were termed 'offside priority designs' and comprise both small and mini island designs.

### Types of roundabout – historical

The types of roundabout were previously classed as:

- *Conventional.*  Weaving sections around a circular or asymmetrical central island. Approaches not normally flared.
- *Small.*  Small central island (4–25 m diameter) with flared approaches to allow multiple vehicle entry.
- *Mini*  Small central island (*less* than 4 m diameter) flush or slightly raised above road (not kerbed), with or without flared approaches. Used at existing junctions in urban areas where approach speeds are less than 60 kph and there is insufficient space for a small roundabout.

Historically, the large roundabouts were designed in relation to the required length of weaving section between entry arms. With the introduction of offside priority, a different design approach emerged. Consequently, for a time, there were two design methods available for roundabouts. The geometric principles of these designs evolved as a result of differently perceived operational mechanisms: weaving, for the 'conventional' roundabouts, and gap-acceptance for the 'offside priority' designs.

# Types of roundabout

The principle objective of a roundabout is to secure a safe interchange of traffic between crossing and weaving traffic streams, with minimum delay.

The approach to roundabout design was reviewed as greater experience was gained of the offside priority designs. It was found that there was no need for the former distinction between 'conventional' and 'small' roundabouts in terms of capacity prediction or otherwise. Consequently, the two former classes of 'conventional' and 'small' roundabout were grouped into a new single class, termed 'normal'. During the 1980s the Department of Transport published revised guidance for the design of roundabouts, based upon operational experience and research of the preceding decade. This was further revised in 1993 (Department of Transport, 1993).

Three main types of roundabout are now defined, namely:

- *Normal.*   One-way around a kerbed central island of at least 4 m diameter; usually flared approaches (to allow multiple vehicle entry).
- *Mini.*   One-way around a flush or slightly raised circular marking of less than 4 m diameter; with or without flared approaches.
- *Double.*   Individual junction with two normal or mini roundabouts, either contiguous or connected by a central link road or kerbed island.

Types of roundabout which are variants of the above are defined as:

- *Grade separated.*   Roundabout which has at least one entry road via an interconnecting slip road from a road at a different level (e.g. underpasses, flyovers, multiple level intersections).
- *Ring junction.*   The usual clockwise one-way circulation of vehicles around a large island is replaced by two-way circulation, with three-arm roundabouts and/or traffic signals at the junction of each approach arm with the circulatory carriageway.
- *Signalized roundabout.*   Roundabout with traffic signals installed on one or more of the approach arms.

## Normal roundabouts

The recommended number of entries is either three or four. Roundabouts with three arms perform especially well and can be more efficient than traffic signals, provided the traffic demand is well balanced between the arms. If the number of entries exceeds four, then the roundabout tends to become larger. This results in possible increased land take, as well as increased probability of higher circulatory speeds within the roundabout (this being undesirable).

### Mini roundabouts

Mini roundabouts are for use in existing urban situations, where constraints preclude the provision of a larger roundabout design. They should only be employed where there is a 30 mph speed limit on all approach arms. The layout design should ensure that drivers have good advance warning of their approach to the mini roundabout. It may well be that physical deflection is not possible on the approach, and in this case road markings and small deflection islands should be used to induce some vehicle deflection, to assist reduction of vehicle speeds and to discourage the straight across manoeuvre over the central circular marking.

### Double roundabouts

These can be useful in a variety of circumstances, including:

- improvement of an existing staggered junction (avoiding the need to realign one of the approach roads and consequently being cost-effective),
- unusual or asymmetrical junctions (e.g. scissors junction), where a single roundabout would require extensive realignment of approaches or excessive land take,
- joining of two parallel routes separated by physical feature (e.g. motorway, railway, river),
- existing crossroads – enables separation of opposing right turn manoeuvres, with these vehicles passing nearside to nearside (contiguous double roundabout),
- overloaded single roundabouts; a double roundabout may reduce circulating flow past critical entries and thereby increase capacity,
- junctions with more than four entries; may achieve increased capacity with lower speeds than a large single roundabout and less land take.

Where a double roundabout layout utilizes mini roundabouts, the stipulation applies that all approaches should be subject to a 30 mph speed limit.

### Grade separated

The most common forms of grade separated roundabout are the *two bridge* type and the *dumbell* (one bridge connecting two roundabouts). A grade separated roundabout solution lends itself to stage construction.

### Ring junctions

There is some experience of unusual types of roundabouts, for example ring junctions, working well at existing junctions which were experiencing operational difficulties. The conversion to a ring junction can be a cost-effective solution for very large roundabouts (perhaps from the era of the large conventional type roundabout designed to accommodate weaving, prior to the offside priority rule) which have entry problems. For this type of junction, which is not widely familiar to drivers, it is especially important that the signing is carefully designed.

### Signalized roundabouts

There is increasing use of traffic signals at roundabouts; these may operate on a 'continuous' or 'part-time' basis. Part-time operation is fairly common, say during morning and/or evening weekday peak periods. The introduction of such traffic signals may be justified when the roundabout form of control operates well for most of the time, but difficulties occur at specific times. Signals are usually introduced so that traffic on arms which are having to give way to a very predominant circulating traffic flow can benefit from forced opportunities to enter the roundabout; in other words, the self-regulating nature of the roundabout junction is not able to function.

## Geometric parameters

Figure 8.1 illustrates the geometric parameters of a roundabout, as defined by the Department of Transport. These are:

v    Approach road half-width.
e    Entry width. Measured perpendicular to the nearside kerbline, from A which is the point of maximum entry deflection at the right-hand end of the give-way line where it meets the median island (or marking).
l'   Average effective length over which the flare is developed. Figure 8.1b illustrates the measurement of l'. CF (the length of l') is parallel to BG and is therefore usually curved, with the length measured along the curve.
D    Inscribed circle diameter.
φ    Entry angle. Serves as a geometric proxy for the conflict angle between entering and circulating streams.
     If less than 30 m between offsides of an entry and next exit, see Fig. 8.1c or 8.1d.
     Otherwise, see Fig. 8.1e. Then $\phi = 90 - (GLB/2)$.
r    Entry radius. Measured as a minimum radius of curvature of the nearside kerbline at entry.

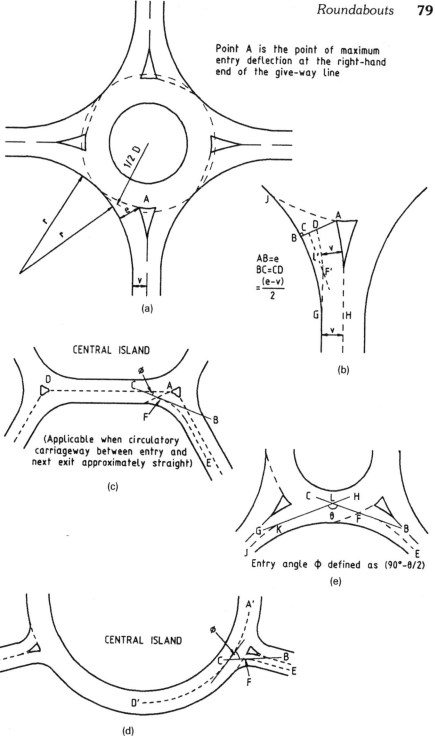

Point A is the point of maximum
entry deflection at the right-hand
end of the give-way line

$AB = e$
$BC = CD$
$= \dfrac{(e-v)}{2}$

(a)

(b)

CENTRAL ISLAND

(Applicable when circulatory
carriageway between entry and
next exit approximately straight)

(c)

Entry angle φ defined as (90°−θ/2)

(e)

CENTRAL ISLAND

(d)

**Fig. 8.1** Roundabout geometric parameters.

# Capacity

## Entry/circulating flow relationship

Each approach arm of a roundabout junction has a capacity. The capacity of the roundabout as a whole is a function of the capacities of the individual entry arms. The operation of the roundabout as a whole can be calculated on the basis that the entries to the roundabout are linked by the common circulating carriageway.

The entry capacity is the maximum inflow from an entry when the demand flow is sufficient to cause steady queuing in the approach. Because of the offside priority rule, entry capacity decreases if circulating flow increases. Therefore, entry capacity must be specified at each level of circulating flow. The dependence of entry flow on circulating capacity is known as the *entry/circulating flow relationship*.

The approach adopted for predicting capacity, and hence performance, of a roundabout is empirically based. This means that the formula used to model the behaviour of a roundabout is derived from data of observed performance of roundabouts. The alternative approach, of developing a theoretically based model, has not to date been adopted. This is because of the difficulty encountered to date in developing a theoretical model which performs satisfactorily.

Of necessity, an empirically-based model is derived using data which extends over specific value ranges for each of the parameters included in the model. Therefore, it does not necessarily follow that the derived model is applicable if parameter values are used which lie outside the observed ranges. Thus, use of the formula representing the entry capacity and circulating flow relationship should be carefully considered when parameter values lie outside the recommended ranges.

## Geometric parameters

The effects on capacity of the geometric factors fall into a distinct hierarchy. The entry width (e) and the flare length (l') have by far the greatest influence; the inscribed circle diameter (D) has a small but important effect; the entry angle ($\phi$) and the radius of entry (r) contribute minor corrections.

## At-grade roundabouts

When all the arms of the roundabout are in the same plane, that is, none of the arms go over or under the roundabout, this is termed 'at-grade'. The entry/circulating flow relationship is defined as:

$$Q_e = F_i - F_iQ_c \qquad \text{when } f_iQ_c \not< F \qquad (8.1)$$

$$Q_e = 0 \text{ when } f_iQ_c > F$$

where    $Q_e$  = entry flow (pcu/h)
             $Q_C$ = circulating flow across the entry (pcu/h)
             $F_i$  = kF
             k   = $1 - 0.00347 (\phi - 30) - 0.978[(1/r) - 0.05]$
             F   = $303 x_2$
             $f_i$   = $kf_c$
             $f_c$   = $0.210 t_D(1 + 0.2x_2)$
             $t_D$  = $1 + 0.5/[1 + \exp[(D - 60)/10)]$
             $x_2$  = $v + (e-v)/(1 + 2S)$
             S   = $1.6 (e-v)/I'$

Whilst, at first glance, the above formulae may seem complex, all values required as input are either geometric parameters of the roundabout (v, e, I', D, $\phi$ and r, as defined above), or the circulating flows on the roundabout (which are derived from the entry flows on each approach).

With respect to the circulating flow for an entry, this is the flow passing the entry arm, and hence the traffic flow to which the entry arm traffic must give way. This is derived as illustrated in Fig. 8.2. In this example of a four arm roundabout, the circulating flow $Q_c$ at Arm A is calculated by:

$$Q_c = q_{D-B} + q_{D-C} + q_{C-B} \qquad (8.2)$$

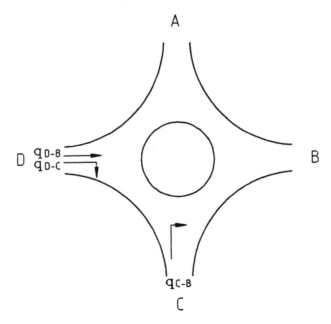

**Fig. 8.2**   Circulating flow.

It is this volume of circulating traffic in which the entry arm must find suitable gaps to enter the roundabout.

### Grade separated roundabouts

When the roads intersecting at a roundabout do not all meet at a common level, the roundabout is 'grade separated'. Research into the operation of grade separated roundabouts has shown that all arms of a grade separated roundabout have a different capacity relationship from that applied to arms of at-grade roundabouts. In this context, a roundabout is defined as grade separated if it connects with a trunk road or motorway type road passing under or over it, or if it connects directly with a motorway type road. Additionally, if a roundabout is very large (maximum overall diameter exceeds 130 m), it should be modelled as grade separated (for analysis purposes).

The entry/circulating flow relationship for modelling a grade separated roundabout is defined as:

$$Q_e = 1.004F - 0.036 \, SEP - 0.232 \, Q_c + \qquad (8.3)$$
$$14.35 - f_c Q_c (2.14 - 0.023 Q_c) \qquad pcu/min$$

where F and $f_c$ are as $F_i$ and $f_i$ in Equation (8.1).

$Q_c$ is the mean circulating flow past the arm under consideration for the central 30 minutes of the total modelled period. SEP is relevant only for arms consisting of separate entry and exit slip roads. It is the separation between the point where the arm enters the roundabout and the point at which the same arm leaves the roundabout. For other arms no value is entered and SEP equals zero.

In general, for grade separated roundabouts, the entry capacity in the absence of circulating traffic is larger, but the entry capacity decreases more rapidly as circulating traffic increases, compared with at-grade roundabouts.

## Analysis methods

### Manual

It is not recommended that the entry flow calculation is undertaken manually. This is primarily because of the much greater time taken for calculation to achieve the comparable level of analysis compared with computation. It should also be noted that manual calculation necessitates the application of a factor to the calculated value of:

$$Q_c = 1.125 \; Q_c \qquad \text{(manual calculations only)} \qquad (8.4)$$

This is to allow for short term variations in traffic flow. The computer programs available for analysing roundabouts adequately model the traffic flows to take account of this. Also, queue length predictions can not be undertaken manually.

## Measures of roundabout performance

The measure commonly used to assess the performance of a roundabout entry arm is referred to as the *RFC*; this is the ratio of the demand traffic flow to the capacity. The demand traffic flow is observed for existing situations in time (traffic counts, see Chapter 5). Future year traffic flows are estimated in accordance with the procedure outlined in Chapter 5; observed traffic flow data are factored to future design year flow estimates using the Department of Transport NRTF factors as appropriate, or other local factors as available. The entry capacity is calculated/computed based upon the entry and circulating flow relationship.

Common engineering practice, (as recommended by the Department of Transport), is to consider a RFC value of 0.85 as the upper desirable value, for operation to acceptable standards of a junction approach arm.

The queue lengths on an entry arm can often be critical in operational terms. For example, if a roundabout is located near to another junction, the queue of vehicles on a roundabout entry arm should not extend to a distance which affects the working of the adjacent junction.

## Computer program: ARCADY

The most commonly used computer program for analysing roundabouts is the Department of Transport's ARCADY. This has a number of features available, including tabulation of predicted RFC values, queue lengths and delays for a defined time period. The selected time period is modelled in user-specified time segments (say, 15 minutes).

The program has a number of optional features, such as accident prediction and the facility to specify a 'queue marker' on an entry arm. If the queue marker option is stipulated, the program output reports the probability of the queue extending back to the queue marker or beyond, for each time segment of the period modelled. This probability can be converted into estimated number of days per year that the queue will reach the marker.

The program can take account of the effect of a pedestrian crossing located close to a roundabout; such a crossing may reduce the vehicular capacity of the roundabout.

# Safety

## *Speed*

Excessive speed, both at entry and within the roundabout, is the most common problem affecting the safety of vehicles at roundabouts. A number of factors can contribute to this and should be avoided, these include:

- inadequate entry deflection,
- very acute entry angle (encourages fast merging),
- poor visibility to the 'give way' line,
- poorly designed or positioned warning and advance direction signs,
- where provided, incorrect siting of 'reduce speed now' signs.

Entry deflection is one of the most important determinants of safety at roundabouts; this is especially important if vehicle speeds are high. For new roundabout schemes, if possible, the arms should be staggered to assist provision of adequate entry deflection. This also tends to reduce the size of roundabout (and hence perhaps landtake). The central island may not provide sufficient entry deflection in urban areas. In such cases, deflection may be generated by the use of enlarged deflection islands, or by subsidiary traffic deflection islands in the entry.

## *Two-wheel vehicles*

Two-wheel vehicles have proved to be significantly more at risk at roundabouts than other vehicles. The particular difficulties encountered by pedal cyclists at roundabouts are of special concern because of the vulnerability of these travellers. Ways of helping pedal cyclists to more safely traverse roundabouts are being explored; research has been sponsored by the Department of Transport and others.

# Practical points of design

The analysis discussed in the foregoing relates to capacity prediction. This can be a most useful aid in the achievement of a good roundabout design. However, in the overall design process a number of other factors, which are not included in the capacity analysis procedure, must also be taken into account. These factors include:

- standards of visibility
- entry width and deflection criteria
- space requirements for large flows of heavy vehicles
- crossfall and drainage

- lighting provision
- use of signs, road markings and road furniture
- surface characteristics of the central island
- aesthetic considerations.

Most of the above factors are especially important in providing a roundabout design which can operate with safety, as referred to previously.

For example, considering entry width and deflection criteria: the offside lane should be deflected so as not to follow a path leading into the central island. A new three-arm roundabout is a common means of providing access to a development from an existing highway (forming two arms of the new roundabout), with the new site access forming the third arm. In such a case it is essential to provide adequate deflection for the straight ahead traffic on the existing highway, (travelling in the lane(s) on the opposite side of the roundabout to the third leg), otherwise there is a danger that this traffic stream will not see the central island and will assume the old highway arrangement of simple two-way traffic along a highway link, thereby not 'giving way' as required at the roundabout.

It is possible to undertake a desk exercise of 'designing' a roundabout, say using ARCADY to quantify the geometric parameter values, and yet that design may not be capable of construction (in the specified required location) to provide a roundabout which meets the overall required standards of design. The design process should be interactive, between capacity analysis and scale drawing of the roundabout, taking account of *all* relevant factors.

With respect to practical design, the following provide some useful guides:

- *Entry width, e*
  Add at least one but not more than two extra lane widths at entry
  Maximum 10.5 m      for single carriageway approach roads
  Maximum 15.0 m      for dual carriageway approach roads

  Minimum 3 m at give-way line (taper back in entry flare to minimum 2 m). It is generally better to provide wider lane widths rather than an additional lane with all lanes very narrow

- *Effective flare length, l'*
  Maximum 100 m
  Minimum 5 m (urban)
  25 m gives good design for rural situations

  Values of l' exceeding 30 or 40 m should be treated with increasing caution (research database had flare lengths up to 27 m only)
  Total length of entry widening is approximately 2l'

- *Entry angle,* φ
  Between 20° and 60°, but 30° is best

- *Entry radius*, r
  Between 6 m and 100 m
  20 m provides good practical design
  If a lot of heavy vehicles, r not less than 10 m

- *Inscribed circle diameter*, D
  Mini roundabout: not more than 28 m (by definition)
  Normal roundabout: not less than 28 m (by definition)

  *Note*   Because of HGV swept path, the entry deflection requirement is difficult to meet if D less than 40 m

- *Circulatory carriageway* around roundabout:
  Circular if possible
  Width constant
  Width 1.0–1.2 times greatest entry width
  Maximum 15 m

- *Exit*
  Exit nearside kerb radius about 40 m at mouth of exit, but not less than 20 m or greater than 100 m.
  Exit wider at the beginning than width of downstream link.

### Understanding and commonsense

In designing a roundabout it is important to always try and understand the reasons for the roundabout behaviour and performance being predicted by the capacity analysis procedure. In so doing, any drawbacks or particular features of the analysis method should be noted. For example, the capacity analysis method described herein is empirical. This means, therefore, that there is no theoretical basis for extending the applicability of the design method beyond the value range of parameters used in deriving the model formula.

In interpreting the results output from the capacity analysis procedure, the value of applying common sense cannot be overstated. In the event of the analysis predicting that, for given levels of traffic demand, the roundabout will not perform satisfactorily, the causal explanation of why this is so should be sought. In this way, the best engineering solution to the capacity difficulty is likely to be identified.

For example, there may be unbalanced demand on the approach arms. Assume that demand from one arm, say arm A, is so overwhelming that the subsequent arm, say arm B, (which has to give way to traffic from arm

A), has little opportunity to find gaps in the circulating flow, and so enter the roundabout. In this case, although the capacity analysis output may suggest that increasing the entry width on Arm B 'makes the roundabout work' to acceptable standards, this may not be the appropriate solution. This may be particularly so if the demand flow on arm B is very low and does not justify a very large multiple entry width, (compared with the existing approach road half-width, which is adequate for the levels of flow on arm B).

A rigid approach to finding design solutions should be avoided. This is illustrated by considering the above example, where it may be that introduction of part-time signals on the roundabout can provide a better solution, compared with providing on arm B additional entry width which is not needed per se, but is rather being provided to address the problem of inadequate gaps in circulating flow during peak periods.

Another example of where signals on a roundabout may be appropriate is in the case of an exit slip road from a motorway joining a grade separated roundabout. If the exit slip road traffic cannot enter the roundabout, due to the heavy circulating flow, then excessive queues may build up on the exit slip road. This can cause interference to the free flow of traffic on the motorway, with adverse implications for both road safety and vehicle delay.

In general, when capacity analysis predicts operational difficulties at a roundabout, the key point is to identify the contributing causal mechanism(s). It is important to consider alternative solutions as appropriate. For developments it is particularly relevant to take account of land ownerships and landtake associated with alternative solutions, and of course cost implications. Similarly, location of the plant of statutory undertakers should be identified and considered when preparing the proposed roundabout layout.

## Checklist

### Types of roundabout
- *Normal*
  - Central island not less than 4 m diameter.
  - Inscribed circle diameter not less than 28 m.
- *Mini*
  - Central island less than 4 m diameter.
  - Inscribed circle diameter not more than 28 m.
  - Approach speeds limited to 30 mph.
  - Existing urban situations.
- *Double*
  - Individual junction with two roundabouts, either contiguous or connected by a central link road or kerbed island

- Variations of the above include: *grade separated, ring junctions and signalized* roundabouts.

### Capacity

- For a given roundabout entry, capacity is a function of geometry and circulating flow (past roundabout entry); defined by the empirically derived entry/circulating flow relationship.
- Entry width (e) and flare length (I') are the geometric parameters with the greatest influence on capacity.
- Grade separated roundabouts have a modified entry and circulating flow relationship (compared with at-grade roundabouts).
- ARCADY is the Department of Transport computer program used to analyse performance of roundabouts.

### Safety

- Excessive speed at entry is the most common safety problem at roundabouts. The most important determinant of safety at roundabouts is the entry deflection.
- Two wheel vehicles are more at risk at roundabouts than other vehicles.

### Practical design

- Understanding of the operational mechanisms in play at the roundabout greatly assists the formulation of a practical design. Other practical design factors excluded from the capacity analysis must be included in the considerations of the design process, including for example, visibility, entry width and deflection and crossfall and drainage.
- Land ownerships and landtake of the proposed solution should be carefully considered, as should location of the plant of statutory undertakers.

## References

Department of Transport (1993) TD 16/93, Geometric Design of Roundabouts, Department of Transport, London.

# Chapter 9
# Traffic Signals

## General

Traffic signal control at a junction reduces the conflict between traffic streams. The aim of good traffic signal design is to optimize traffic throughput at the junction whilst addressing the objective of improved highway safety. This includes giving full consideration to the needs and demand for pedestrian flow at the junction.

Traffic signals are the most common form of control for important junctions within an urban highway network. The widespread use of traffic signal control can be attributed to a number of factors, including:

- signals make the most effective use of roadspace where development is intense,
- signals provide inherent flexibility in coping with variable and changing traffic patterns,
- signals can be coordinated on an area-wide basis, so as to minimize overall delays through a highway network (known as urban traffic control, UTC),
- signal junctions are usually safer for pedestrians than other forms of junction control, as positive pedestrian crossing periods can be provided within the signal stage sequence.

## Traffic signals and development proposals

Consideration of traffic signal control is frequently a requirement in respect of development proposals. Presented below are some typical examples of situations which can arise:

- Traffic signal control may be a preferred option for the proposed access junction to serve the development.
- One or more of the existing junctions on the highway network local to the development site may presently operate under traffic signal control. Traffic generated by the development will pass through the existing signal junction(s). The impact upon the operational perfor-

mance of the existing signal junction (of the traffic generated by the development proposal) must be assessed. How much development generated traffic can be accommodated by the existing traffic signal junction? Can the performance of the signal junction be improved by amending signal timings and/or improving the junction geometry? How much extra traffic can the improved signal junction accommodate?

- Traffic generated by the development will pass through existing junction(s) on the highway network which do not presently operate under traffic signal control, (they may for example operate as major/minor priority junctions). If traffic signal control is introduced at these existing off-site junctions then the development generated traffic may be satisfactorily accommodated.
- Introduction of linked traffic signal control at several existing major/minor priority control junctions in the locale of the development site can enable traffic generated by the development to be accommodated in an acceptable operational manner, with the added benefit of improved road safety.

## Definitions

A certain amount of 'jargon' is used to describe traffic signal operations, and a number of basic terms are defined in the following. Even for those not undertaking traffic signal analysis, an appreciation of this terminology is helpful during discussions of traffic signal junction performance.

### Phases and stages

The sequence of settings on a traffic signal installation can be referred to in two ways: *phase* and *stage*, which may possibly appear confusing. To understand this it is helpful to first define the following terms:

- *Approach* – one or more lanes where the traffic can be considered as forming a single queue.
- *Traffic stream* – traffic on an approach which receives a signalled right-of-way for the same period.

Figure 9.1 illustrates the meaning of the terms *phase* and *stage*.

*Phase* refers to a set of traffic movements which can occur simultaneously: that is, they receive identical signal light indications. Phase is also used to refer to the sequence of signal indications received by such a set of traffic movements. Two or more streams may share the same phase (C on Fig. 9.1).

The term *stage* is concerned with the sequential steps in which junction

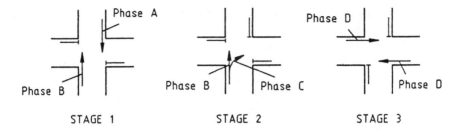

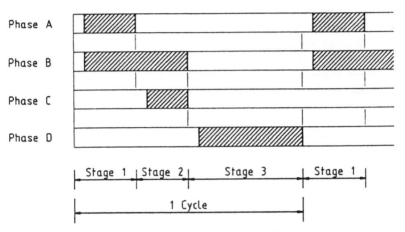

**Fig. 9.1**  Stage and phase control.

control is varied. A stage is that part of the cycle during which a particular set of phases receives green.

### Signal features

There are a further number of basic terms used to describe traffic signal control operations, as listed below:

- *Aspect* indication shown at any one time by a signal face. In the UK the sequence is: red  –  red/amber  –  green  –  amber
                           (2 seconds)                    (3 seconds)
  Permitted options include:
  - green arrow, to assist traffic direction and control (for example, right-turn stage)
  - red and green man, for pedestrians
  - cycle symbols, to assist cyclists.
- *Green time* (k) – period of time a signal shows a green aspect.
- *Intergreen period* (I) – time from end of green period of stage having right-of-way to start of green period of stage gaining right-of-way. In

the UK the minimum available length of intergreen period is four seconds.

- *Cycle time* (c) – complete series of stages.
- *Effective green time* (g) – for each stage. That part of the actual green time (k) + amber time (a) which when multiplied by saturation flow rate (s) gives the maximum number of vehicles that can enter the junction (refer to Fig. 9.2 and 'Saturation flow' below).

## Intergreen period

The intergreen period is the time which occurs between stages when there is no green signal aspect showing on any traffic signal head. The intergreen period is incorporated in the interests of highway safety. Its purpose is to ensure that conflict between traffic streams does not occur in the changeover between right-of-way for conflicting traffic streams. Although the minimum permissible intergreen period is four seconds, safety considerations generally require a longer period:

- to allow vehicles to clear an intersection when the distance across the junction is excessive,
- to improve safety on high speed roads,
- on roads where there are insufficient 'right-turners' to justify a separate stage.

In the latter case the premise is that a vehicle waiting within the junction

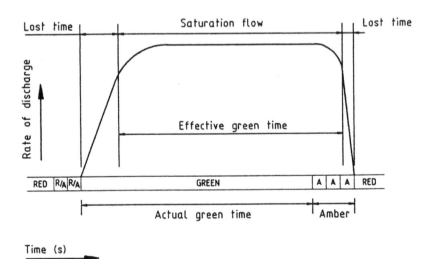

**Fig. 9.2**  Saturation flow.

to complete the right-turn manoeuvre can safely clear the junction during the intergreen period.

In general, if the evergreen period is too short this is potentially dangerous. It is equally unsatisfactory if the intergreen period is too long, as this leads to delay, frustration and disobedience of the signal discipline.

Figure 9.3 provides a guide to determining the desirable length of intergreen. The objective is that a vehicle passing over the stop-line at the start of amber will be clear of a potential collision point, in relation to the vehicle starting at the onset of the green of the following stage, (when travelling at the normal speed for the junction). Referring to Fig. 9.3:

- When the E-W arms losing right-of-way:
  If        (AF) – (BF) > (CH) – (DH)
  then     'x' = (AF) – (BF) or vice versa
- When the N-S arms losing right-of-way:
  If        (BG) – (CG) > (DE) – (AE)
  then     'x' = (BG) – (CG) or vice versa

The required intergreen period can be determined from Table 9.1, for a given value of 'x' for 'ahead traffic' (i.e. straight ahead). However, if there is an appreciable level of right-turning traffic and this is the determining factor in selecting the length of intergreen, then Table 9.2 should be used.

As a point of detail, when the following stage is a pedestrian stage, 'x' should be determined from the position of the pedestrian crossing. If pedestrians are losing right-of-way, the start of the following stage should be delayed until the crossing area is clear.

## Saturation flow

Saturation flow is the maximum rate of discharge which can be sustained (across a signal stop-line) for a traffic stream. Saturation flow can either be

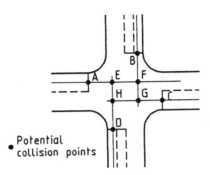

**Fig. 9.3**   Determining I.

**Table 9.1**   Intergreen periods for ahead traffic.

| Distance 'x' metres | Intergreen I seconds |
|---|---|
| 9 | 5 |
| 10–18 | 6 |
| 19–27 | 7 |
| 28–36 | 8 |
| 37–46 | 9 |
| 47–54 | 10 |
| 55–64 | 11 |
| 65–74 | 12 |

**Table 9.2**   Intergreen periods: appreciable right turn traffic.

| Distance 'x' metres | Intergreen I seconds |
|---|---|
| 9 | 5 |
| 10–13 | 6 |
| 14–20 | 7 |
| 21–27 | 8 |
| 28–34 | 9 |
| 35–40 | 10 |
| 41–45 | 11 |
| 46–50 | 12 |

measured (for existing traffic signal installations) or estimated empirically, as outlined below.

Generally, experience of considering traffic signal junctions fosters an ability to roughly estimate saturation flow for different circumstances. For those not so experienced, it is helpful to have some general idea of the value of saturation flow (for a lane) that might be expected. As a rough guide, the saturation flow for a lane of about 3.25 m wide with traffic manoeuvres unopposed may be in the range of about 1800–1950 vehicles per hour, (although it is stressed that this varies depending upon a number of factors, as outlined below). This saturation flow value is the number of vehicles which would pass over the stop line if the lane were to receive a green signal for the complete hour.

There follows some explanation of the factors affecting saturation flow and the methods of estimation of saturation flow value.

## Factors affecting saturation flow

- *Width of lane.*   Generally, saturation flow for a lane increases with width.
- *Number of lanes.*   Saturation flow per lane does not vary with the number of lanes. Saturation flow for the whole stop-line is the sum of the saturation flow for each lane (for permitted movements).
- *Parked cars*, bus stops etc. within lane width available to traffic stream – generally reduce the saturation flow (if located critically in relation to the stop-line).
- Proportion of *turning traffic* within the traffic stream e.g. are there a lot of right-turners?
- *Gradient* on approach lane, up gradients reduce saturation flow, down gradients increase saturation flow.
- *Traffic composition.*

## Estimation of saturation flow: experimentally

A standard procedure for measuring saturation flow is specified (MOT/ RRL, 1963). This involves recording the number of vehicles crossing the stop-line once saturation has been achieved, in time increments of say six seconds. Observations can only take place when the saturation flow rate is achieved; in other words there must be a steady stream of vehicles demanding to cross the stop-line, with no gaps in flow. This makes it difficult to measure saturation flow for some traffic streams, as even at a very busy junction there can be a particular traffic stream which does not experience demand flows at saturation levels over a significant time period.

## Estimation of saturation flow: empirically

Formulae for predicting the saturation flows at traffic signal controlled junctions have been derived from field studies and simulation, (described in RR67 (TRRL, 1986)). The main factors which affect the estimated value of saturation flow are:

- traffic intensity on opposing arm, (this affects the number of gaps available for turning traffic),
- number of storage spaces available within the junction which right-turners can use without blocking straight ahead traffic,
- number of signal cycles per hour.

The empirical formulae for predicting saturation flows are not included herein as the notation is extensive and the formulae may be considered complex. In the event that empirical estimation of saturation flows is unavoidable, the reader is referred to the *OSCADY User Manual* (Department of Transport, 1989), which includes the formulae and associated worked examples. The formulae are also summarized in Appendix A of RR105 (TRRL, 1987).

Calculation of saturation flows is generally a time consuming task, (although less so than experimentally measuring saturation flow). This may, however, be unavoidable as part of the traffic impact analysis for a proposed development. For example, a TRANSYT (TRRL, 1980) analysis requires as explicit input the saturation flow values for each traffic stream, (TRANSYT is the computer program used to analyse linked traffic signal networks, further information is provided later in this chapter). On the other hand, the computer program OSCADY computes internally the estimated saturation flow for a lane, based on geometric data provided (OSCADY is the computer program used to analyse isolated traffic signal junctions, further information is provided later in this chapter).

### Traffic composition

Vehicle size and type has an effect upon the movement of vehicles across the stop-line. For example, heavy goods vehicles (HGVs) do not have the same acceleration and manoeuvrability as the average car, and therefore, in a given time period and under saturated traffic flow demand conditions, less HGVs can cross the stop-line than would cars.

To take account of this the concept of *passenger car units* (pcu) is applied. This is where each vehicle type is considered in terms of the passenger car unit equivalent. Table 9.3 summarizes the pcu factors for different vehicle types.

**Table 9.3**   pcu factors for traffic signals.

| Vehicle type | pcu Value[1] |
|---|---|
| Car | 1.0 |
| HGV[2] | 2.3 |
| MGV[3] | 1.5 |
| Bus | 2.0 |
| Motorcycle | 0.4 |
| Pedal cycle | 0.2 |

*Notes*
(1) pcu is passenger car unit
(2) HGV is heavy goods vehicle
(3) MGV is medium goods vehicle.

# Traffic signal capacity

A traffic signal junction is analysed to estimate or predict the operational performance with demand flows which are expected to occur. In the case of development proposals this permits an assessment of whether the traffic impact of the development can be acceptably accommodated by the traffic signal junction being analysed and what measures, if any, are required as a consequence of the development.

It is recommended that traffic signal analysis is undertaken using computer programs available for the purpose. Design of traffic signal timings for a junction operating with demand near to capacity is not recommended for the novice, necessarily involving a good understanding of the alternative ways of accommodating traffic demands by different signal stagings and special facilities. It is also stressed that a practical understanding of the way in which traffic behaves is required; an overly optimistic view of the way in which traffic will manoeuvre at the junction can lead to a misleading output from analysis.

There follows some explanation of key components with respect to capacity analysis.

## Right-turning traffic

Right-turning traffic may have the following effects on traffic flow:

- Right-turn traffic is delayed because of opposing flow.
- Right-turn traffic in a particular lane inhibits use of this lane by straight ahead traffic.
- A right-turning vehicle caught beyond the stop-line after the end of a phase completes the manoeuvre and interferes with the start of the next phase.

The four situations which can occur are described in Table 9.4.

**Table 9.4**  Right-turning traffic: situations that can occur.

| Case | Flow | | Exclusive right-turning lane |
|------|------------|---------|-----------------------------|
|      | Unopposed | Opposed |                             |
| (a)  | ✓         |         | Yes                         |
| (b)  | ✓         |         | No                          |
| (c)  |           | ✓       | Yes                         |
| (d)  |           | ✓       | No                          |

### Lost time

The term *lost time* is used in two senses within the context of describing traffic signal operations. This can therefore be confusing, particularly as in both cases lost time refers to time which is effectively not available for traffic to progress through the signal junction.

#### Lost time due to starting delays

Lost time due to starting delays is the term used to describe the time lost due to acceleration and deceleration at the beginning and end of the green period. Note that although this encompasses time at both the start and end of the green time, it is nevertheless referred to as 'lost time due to starting delays'. The defined relationship for lost time due to starting delays is illustrated on Figure 9.2. This is uncorrelated with site factors.

$$l = k + a - g \qquad (9.1)$$

where  $l$  = lost time due to starting delays
       $k$  = green time (seconds)
       $a$  = amber time (3 seconds)
       $g$  = effective green time (seconds).

There is a frequent assumption, for the purposes of calculations, that the value of $l$ is two seconds. Specifically when this is assumed, then the relationship between green time and effective green time becomes:

$$k = g - 1 \text{ seconds} \qquad (9.2)$$

In RR67 (TRRL, 1986) it is reported that, for the sites considered, the component values of the lost time due to starting delays (averaged over the sites) were recorded as:

Starting (acceleration):   mean value 1.35 seconds
                           standard deviation 0.55 seconds
End (deceleration):        mean value 1.1 seconds
                           standard deviation 0.13 seconds.

This equates to an aggregate value of 'lost time due to starting delays' of 2.45 seconds, averaged over the sites.

#### Lost time: total per cycle

The total lost time over a complete signal cycle for a junction is defined by:

$$L = \Sigma l + \Sigma (I - a) \qquad (9.3)$$

where  $L$  = total lost time per cycle
       $l$  = lost time due to starting delays
       $a$  = amber.

Note that (as amber is three seconds, standard), when l is two seconds (actual/assumed), then

$$L = \Sigma \, (I - 1) \tag{9.4}$$

## Cycle time

The optimum cycle time is defined as that cycle time which gives the least average delay to all vehicles using the junction. In practice there may be reasons why the calculated 'optimum cycle time' is not the actual cycle time which is adopted and set on the traffic installation.

Calculation of optimum cycle time is as follows:

Define y as

$$y = \frac{\text{actual flow}}{\text{saturation flow}} = \frac{q}{s} \tag{9.5}$$

$$\text{then} \quad c_o = \frac{1.5 \, L + 5}{1 - y_1 - y_2 \, \ldots \, - y_n} \tag{9.6}$$

$$\text{and so} \quad c_o = \frac{1.5 \, L + 5}{1 - Y} \tag{9.7}$$

where
| | |
|---|---|
| $c_o$ | = cycle time giving minimum delay |
| $y_1, y_2, \ldots y_n$ | = maximum ratios of flow to saturation flow for stages 1 to n |
| Y | = sum of y values for each stage. |

In practice, the maximum cycle time set at signals is 120 seconds, (as there is little gain in efficiency by using longer cycle times). Longer cycle times generally lead to longer queue lengths on an approach, which can be critical, for example in urban situations. As a general guide, minimum delay is not exceeded by more than about 10 to 20% if cycle time is set so that it lies in the range

$$0.75 \, c_o \nless c \nless 1.5 \, c_o \tag{9.8}$$

## Green times

For minimum delay the available effective green time is divided between the phases in proportion to the $y_{max}$ value for each phase.

$$c = L + \Sigma \, g \tag{9.9}$$

Thus for two stage signals:

$$\frac{g_1}{g_2} = \frac{y_1}{y_2} \tag{9.10}$$

$$\text{and so} \quad g_1 = \frac{y_1\,(c - L)}{Y} \tag{9.11}$$

Having calculated the effective green times the actual green times may be determined from Equation (9.1).

### Reserve capacity

Reserve capacity is a measure commonly used to describe the performance of a traffic signal junction. It is a measure of how near to practical capacity the junction is operating.

The maximum possible capacity for any approach is given by:

$$\frac{s\,g}{c} \quad \text{pcu/hour} \tag{9.12}$$

The capacity of the whole junction is dependent upon the total amount of lost time (L) in the cycle. As the practical limit for cycle time is set at 120 seconds (refer above under 'cycle time'), the ultimate capacity of the junction could be calculated as the flow that could just pass through the junction when the signals are set at that cycle time. However, this is the maximum capacity and is associated with long delays. It is more usual to work to a *practical capacity* of 90% of the maximum, resulting in shorter delays.

$$\text{Define} \quad c_m = \frac{L}{1 - Y} \tag{9.13}$$

where   $c_m$ = minimum cycle time, i.e. cycle time theoretically just long enough to pass through the junction all traffic that arrives in the cycle.

Hence   $Y = 1 - L/c_m$

Since the maximum permissible value of $c_m = 120$ seconds, and $Y_{practical} = 0.9\,Y$, then

$$Y_{practical} = 0.9\,(1 - L/120)$$

i.e.   $Y_{practical} = 0.9 - 0.0075\,L \tag{9.14}$

is the limiting case
Thus at existing flow:

$$Reserve\ capacity = \frac{(Y_{practical} - Y)\,100}{Y} \quad \text{per cent} \tag{9.15}$$

## Design of isolated traffic signal junctions

Manual traffic signal calculations are not recommended as this does not generally permit the degree of sophistication achieved with computer analysis, and takes a much greater length of time to achieve the comparable level of analysis as undertaken by computation.

### Measures of traffic signal junction performance

The measure commonly used to assess the performance of a traffic stream (at a traffic signal junction) is referred to as the *RFC*; this is the ratio of the demand traffic flow to the capacity. The demand traffic flow is observed for existing situations in time. Future year traffic flows are estimated in accordance with the procedures outlined in Chapter 5. Observed traffic flow data are factored to future design year flow estimates using the Department of Transport NRTF factors as appropriate, or other local factors as available.

Common engineering practice, as recommended by the Department of Transport, is to consider a RFC value of 0.85 as the upper desirable value, for operation to acceptable standards of a junction approach lane.

The queue length on an approach can often be critical in operational terms; for example, if it is likely to extend back to block an adjacent junction or significant access, such as a fire station exit. This should be taken into account when assessing the acceptability of junction arrangements for anticipated traffic demands.

The *reserve capacity* of the traffic signal junction provides an indication of the measure of additional traffic which the junction might accommodate and still operate to acceptable standards. Reserve capacity is computed in respect of the whole junction, rather than in respect of individual traffic streams or approach lanes.

### Computer program: OSCADY

The most commonly used computer program for analysing individual traffic signal junctions is the Department of Transport's OSCADY (Optimized Signal Capacity and DelaY). OSCADY optimizes signal timings and predicts capacities, queues and delays at isolated signal controlled junctions, providing a valuable tool for the design of new junctions and to assess the effects of modifying existing junctions. Although other computer programs that perform a similar function are available, use of OSCADY is the most widespread.

The basic theory and terms adopted in OSCADY are as described elsewhere in this chapter, for example, saturation flow, optimum cycle time, green times, reserve capacity. A number of features are available, including tabulation of predicted RFC values, queue lengths and delays for a defined time period. The selected time period is modelled in user-specified time segments (say, 15 minutes).

OSCADY has a number of optional features, such as graphical output, which can display the build-up and decay of queues on an approach over the period being modelled.

## Layout of traffic signal junctions

The layout of a traffic signal junction can be constrained by existing features, such as buildings and land ownership. Such constraints may be less severe for new junctions than with existing, for example in the case of a new signal junction to provide the primary access to a development site. However, as with all junctions provided as part of a development proposal, it is essential to ensure that the proposed layout does not require land over which the developer and/or the highway authority does not have control.

The basic components of a traffic signal installation are illustrated by example in Figure 9.4, and outlined in the following paragraphs.

### Primary signal

Location should take account of a number of factors, including:

- swept paths of turning vehicles, critically of large goods vehicles (see Chapter 15: Servicing),
- bus stops and/or bus layby locations,
- pedestrian crossing needs,
- cyclists.

### Duplicate primary signal

A duplicate primary signal is not always required; the following points apply:

- may be required on the offside of a wide approach, or when the visibility of the nearside primary signal is restricted;
- recommended on all high speed roads;
- on two-way roads where a duplicate primary signal is provided it must be sited on a central refuge, and not on the offside of the carriageway;
- on one-way roads where a duplicate primary signal is provided, it must be located on the offside of the road.

### Secondary signal

Additional signals are normally sited beyond the junction, and referred to as secondary signals. These must always display the same information as the primary, but it is permitted to provide additional information which does not conflict with the primary, for example a right-turn arrow.

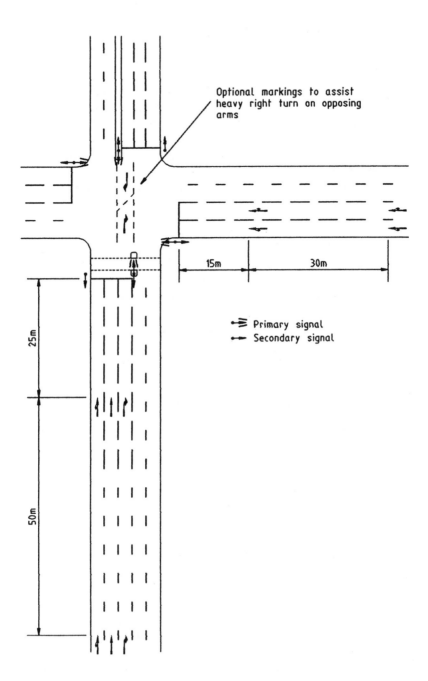

Optional markings to assist
heavy right turn on opposing
arms

15m

30m

25m

50m

Primary signal
Secondary signal

**Fig. 9.4** Typical traffic signal layout.

Circumstances can occur where it is preferable not to locate the secondary signal beyond the junction, for example in association with pedestrian needs and safety at a T-junction. Each case must be carefully considered on its merits, taking account of the practicalities of operation.

### Stop-line

The stop-line is located on the approach to the primary signal, with a distance of between 1.0–2.0 metres between the stop-line and the primary signal.

### Traffic signal controller

The traffic signal controller operates the installation. This can be comparatively sophisticated, (for example for vehicle actuated signals, refer to 'Vehicle actuation' below), or can be relatively basic with the sophistication provided by a central control computer, as in an urban traffic control system, see below for more information.

## Control strategy

Signals may operate under various control methods. These include:

- *fixed time signals*: predetermined signal timings based on historic data,
- *vehicle actuated signals*: responsive to varying traffic conditions, with minimum and maximum timings set,
- *coordinated traffic signals*: several signal junctions linked in operation, to minimize delays over the network. In the simplest case this may involve linking of consecutive traffic signal junctions along a major route and coordinating traffic signal timings, so as to avoid major road vehicles stopping at each junction. In a more complex example, traffic signal junctions over an area are coordinated so as to minimize delays over the area wide network; this is referred to as urban traffic control (UTC).

## Fixed time signals

These operate to a predetermined program in which the length of cycle time and green periods are of fixed duration. These times should be such that minimum delay is caused to vehicle streams passing through a junction. Of necessity, signal timings are computed using historical data (traffic count data collected at some time previously). With fixed time signals the order of stages and timings are not varied to meet changing conditions, and hence delays can be unacceptable, leading to driver frustration and possible disobedience. It is, however, possible to incorporate demand-dependent stages, such as a pedestrian stage.

It is also possible to have a number of fixed time programs for different traffic conditions, each timing program computed using historical traffic count data. Each set of timings is referred to as a signal plan. Thus for example, there may be fixed time signal plans for weekday am peak, weekday pm peak, weekday off-peak, weekend. An automatic timing device is used to implement the change of signal plan.

Generally, in the UK fixed time operation is only used for urban traffic control (UTC) schemes (refer below to the section on 'Urban traffic control').

## Vehicle actuated signals

Time intervals are varied in accordance with traffic demand. Stages may be omitted if there is no requirement. Demand is registered through suitably placed vehicle detectors which are linked to the traffic signal controller. The standard method of detection is to have inductive loops buried in the road surface. Older installations employed a pneumatic tube detector, but this approach is now out-of-date.

In the past, vehicle actuation was the common form of signal control in urban areas. However, the introduction of UTC is increasingly widespread. Nevertheless, there are still many locations at which vehicle actuated signals are in operation.

In any case, vehicle actuation is recommended for *isolated* (uncoordinated) traffic signal control junctions, as providing a satisfactory way to respond to fluctuations in traffic density.

### Facilities

The facilities available for a vehicle actuated signal installation include:

- *Minimum green period* – shortest period of right-of-way given to any stage. Long enough for vehicles waiting between detector and stopline to get into motion and safely clear the junction. Usually in the range 7–10 seconds.

This may be increased by:

- *Vehicle-extension periods* – as each vehicle crosses the detector the green period is extended by an amount (the vehicle extension period). The extension period required for each of the loops is usually 1.5 seconds, based on a minimum approach speed of 20 mph (refer to Figure 9.5). Extensions are individual, not cumulative.

up to:

- *Maximum green period* – pre-set to prevent vehicles on a halted stage from waiting indefinitely. In the peak hour most signals operate to continuous maximum green times, (thus effectively operating as fixed time signals over the peak hour).

Other facilities include:

- *All-red period* – an extended all-red between two traffic stages is *not recommended* (Department of Transport, 1981). This leads to increased delays to traffic and to driver disobedience, since the extended period is always present, even when there is no pedestrian demand.

  The preferred alternative is a full pedestrian stage which is demand-called.

- *Early cut-off* – where there is a heavy right-turn demand on one approach. The green time of the opposing arm is terminated (early cut-off) before the green for the arm containing the right-turns. The early cut-off may be a fixed time period, or detector extended. An early cut-off should *not be used* where there is a single lane approach. When an early cut-off is provided the secondary signal should have a right-turn arrow illuminated during the right-turn time.

- *Late start* – is an alternative method of catering for right-turn vehicles. The start of the green time for the opposing traffic is delayed by a few seconds. This causes difficulty at the start of the following stage if the right-turn demand is heavy, as the opposing flow can not easily establish precedence. For this reason a late start is *not recommended* (Department of Transport, 1981). No green arrows are provided.

## MOVA

The MOVA (Microprocessor Optimized Vehicle Actuation) signal control strategy for isolated traffic signal junctions (TRRL, 1990) has been

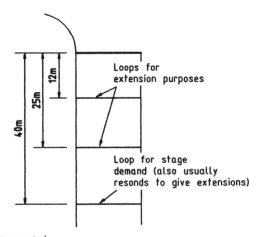

**Fig. 9.5**   Vehicle-extension periods.

developed by the Transport Research Laboratory. The MOVA method is implemented by equipment based upon a microprocessor, which can be connected to modern UK traffic signal controllers. The Department of Transport favour the introduction of MOVA control for isolated traffic signal junctions. The MOVA system is based upon a preset sequence of stages, which receive the green signal provided that the traffic situation satisfies specified conditions for a stage to be 'called'. The MOVA strategy takes full advantage of modern technology to react sensitively to changing traffic conditions. However, the basis of operation is that of the facilities which are available for a traditional vehicle actuated traffic signal installation.

## Coordinated traffic signals

When several signal controlled junctions occur along a major route some form of coordination is required to prevent, as far as possible, the major road vehicles stopping at each junction. Alternatively, or additionally, signals may be coordinated to minimize delays to vehicles. Where storage for queuing vehicles is a particular problem, signals may be linked to prevent queues from one junction extending back to the preceding signals. Linking of signals gives benefits over and above those benefits attributable to the sum of the individually controlled junctions.

Systems for coordinating traffic signals include:

- *Simultaneous* – All signals display the same aspect at the same time. This is only suitable for short signal spacings on routes with a predominant proportion of green time. It has the disadvantage of encouraging drivers to speed so as to avoid being stopped at a change of stage. If turning traffic is light and junctions are closely spaced this system may have advantages for pedestrian movement.
- *Alternate* – This gives an opposite indication at the same time on alternate streets, and is best suited for equal junction spacing at about 300 m intervals. The cycle time must be common to all signals and must be related to speed progression.
- *Double alternate* – This uses quarter-cycle offset.
- *Flexible progressive* – The green periods at adjacent signal junctions are offset relative to each other according to the desired speed on the highway. Progression along the highway in both directions must be considered and this usually results in a compromise between the flow in both directions and also between major and minor road flows.

## Urban Traffic Control (UTC)

A UTC system is one in which a large number of signal junctions are controlled by a single computer; the principles are illustrated in Fig. 9.6.

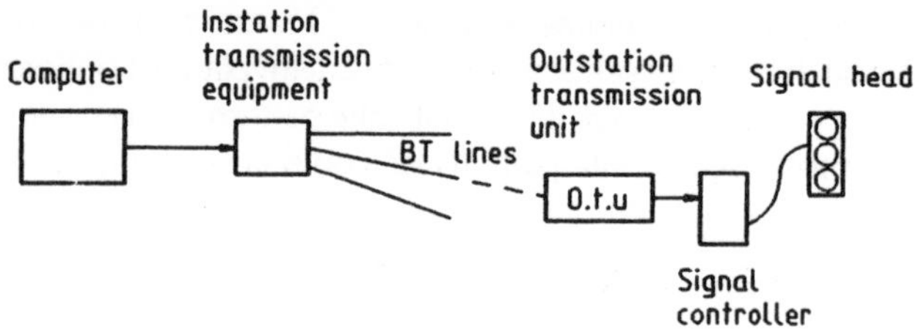

**Fig. 9.6** UTC system (information flow).

A large UTC system has dual computers, whereas a compact UTC system is defined as having a single computer with a maximum of 30 outstation transmission units (OTUs) and, because controllers can share OTUs, a maximum of about 45 controllers. In a UTC system the sophistication is with the computer; the controller is basic.

### Implications of UTC

The main implications of installing a UTC system for a highway network are:

- All main pedestrian and traffic junctions operating on a give way basis must be brought under signal control.
- All signals in particular controlled areas must have the same cycle time (or multiple thereof).
- Coordination of signals on a common cycle time is arranged to minimize delays to traffic and pedestrians.

### Objectives of UTC

Some of the objectives are:

- signal coordination (library of time plans)
- equipment monitoring
- bus priority
- emergency vehicle priority
- collection of traffic data
- diversions and variable signing
- queue indication
- car park information data.

### Signal coordination

This is the most important function of a UTC system. The timings of the signals under control are coordinated so as to minimize overall delay to traffic over the highway network. Measured flow and journey times through the network are used to calculate plans of optimum signal timings and offsets which suit different traffic patterns. The computer implements the most appropriate plan, usually on a time of day or day of week basis.

### Methods used for implementing UTC

There are two methods of control which are used in the UK. These are similar in concept but differ in terms of the input data. The methods referred to are known as TRANSYT and SCOOT and are described below. The fundamental difference between TRANSYT and SCOOT is that TRANSYT calculates signal timing plans based on historical traffic data, whereas SCOOT uses on-line dynamic traffic flow data to update and amend signal timings.

## TRANSYT

The method most used in the UK for calculating the optimum signal settings is the Transport Research Laboratory computer program TRANSYT (TRAffic Network StudY Tool). The fixed time signal plans produced are based on *historical* data, that is data previously recorded (for example, traffic flows in the morning peak hour). The method assumes that all signals to be coordinated will operate on a common cycle time (or half that cycle time) and that all flows, saturation flows and average link journey times in the network are known.

Use of TRANSYT to optimize traffic signal timings over a network can be expected to result in significant savings in vehicle delays over the network, as well as road safety benefits.

The program has two main elements

- Traffic model – used to calculate the *performance index* of the network for a given set of signal timings,
- Hill climbing optimisation process – makes changes to the settings and determines whether or not they improve the performance index.

### Performance index

The performance index is computed for each TRANSYT run of the network being analysed, and is included in the program output. The lower the performance index, the more efficiently the signal network is operating. This can be appreciated by reference to the definition of performance index:

$$\text{Performance index} = \sum_{i=1}^{n} (d_i + K\, c_i) \qquad (9.16)$$

where   $d_i$ = average network delay (vehicle hours per hour) on $i^{th}$ link
of network

$c_i$ = average number of vehicle stops per second on $i^{th}$ link of
network

K = weighting factor chosen by operator.

(The value of K can vary on individual links; it is not necessary to set an
overall value for the network. A reasonable average value is 10).

### Platoon flow and dispersion

Benefits will only be obtained from linking traffic signals if there are
platoon arrivals. The principle is that traffic arriving at a signal stop-line
and passing through the junction (on green) travels as a group (platoon) to
the next signal junction and also progresses through that signal junction
as a group (platoon).

There will be some dispersion of the platoon as it progresses along the
link between the downstream and upstream signal junctions, due to
differing speeds of vehicles within the platoon. In congested traffic
conditions the opportunity for a vehicle to travel at a speed significantly
different from the average speed of the platoon is limited by constraints
imposed by the prevailing traffic conditions. Figure 9.7 illustrates the
typical platoon dispersion which occurs when traffic discharges during a
fully saturated green period.

Indeed, one of the advantages of introducing TRANSYT control is that
it encourages regular platoon travel because the green times of consecutive signal junctions are set in relation to a design speed of travel
progression along the highway link. Thus, if a vehicle travels at a speed
significantly greater than this design speed, it is likely to arrive at the next
signal stopline before the green aspect is available. Therefore, there is no
advantage in travelling at a speed greater than the design speed and thus
platoon travel is encouraged and reinforced. This has various advantages,
including safety aspects. For example, with platoon travel it is easier and
safer for pedestrians to judge and undertake safe crossing of roads.

If the distance between signals is so great that the platoon disperses to
the extent that arrivals are virtually random, that is a good place to split
for sub-areas of the TRANSYT network. A complete network is split into
sub-areas such that all signals within a sub-area have the same cycle time.
Anything that will constitute a significant disruption to the platoon flow
must either be removed, for example, a zebra crossing converted to
pelican crossing, or must constitute a definition of sub-areas, for example,
a roundabout cannot be included within a sub-area.

## SCOOT

The SCOOT (Split Cycle and Offset Optimization Techniques) computer
program uses a specially developed algorithm to analyse raw detector

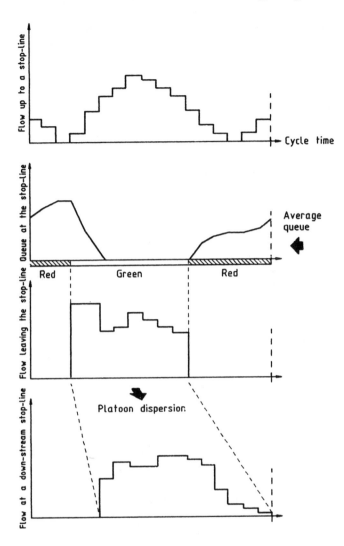

*Source* DoE/DOT/TRRL (1975) Report LR 888 *User Guide to TRANSYT Version 8*

**Fig. 9.7** Platoon dispersion.

data and thence define signal timings in real time: thus signal timings are based on dynamic data.

### Aims of SCOOT

The aims of SCOOT are:

- to reduce vehicle delay, stops and congestion to levels below those achieved by the best fixed time system (TRANSYT),

- to remove the need for updating fixed time plans,
- to provide information for traffic management purposes.

### Dynamic data

Inductive loop detectors are located on all approaches to signalized junctions under SCOOT control. Detectors should be positioned as far upstream from the signal stop-line as possible; usually a detector can be placed at the exit of the upstream junction. Each loop has to be calibrated to the model. Figure 9.8 illustrates the flow of information in a SCOOT UTC system.

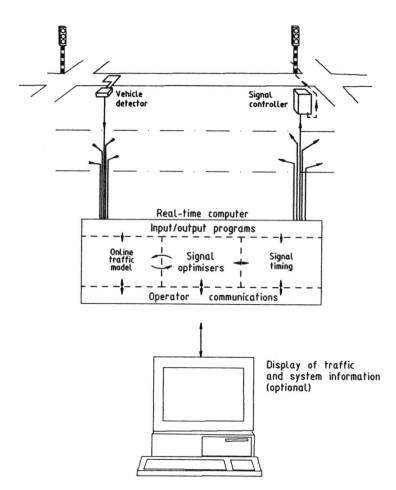

**Fig. 9.8**   SCOOT system (information flow).

### Operation of SCOOT

SCOOT operates groups of adjacent junctions on a common cycle time. At any instant the cycle time, green durations and offsets between signals are controlled by timings held in the computer store.

The traffic model uses dynamic data to predict the total delay and stops caused by signal timings. The signal optimizer adjusts the timings to reduce this total. Frequent small alterations adapt the signals to short term fluctuations in travel demand. Longer term trends are satisfied by the accumulation of small alterations over several minutes. Thus there are no large sudden changes in timings to disrupt traffic flow.

## Comparison of TRANSYT and SCOOT

TRANSYT operates using historical data and thus there is a limited life span to the timing plans which are calculated (as traffic flows and patterns change over time). SCOOT does not suffer from this problem and further is able to provide up-to-date traffic information which may be used for a variety of purposes. SCOOT has been demonstrated to offer additional reductions in delay time savings over the network, over and above those achieved with a TRANSYT network.

SCOOT is primarily a control strategy, and as such does not replace conventional UTC systems, rather it works with them. The 'kernel' SCOOT software starts with the analysis of raw detector data and ends with recommendation of signal timings. All the standard UTC functions for example, data transmission, fault monitoring, are still required to make up a complete system. SCOOT may be thought of as a 'black box' within, or attached to, a conventional UTC system.

A fundamental advantage of SCOOT is that it offers the ability to provide responsive traffic signal timings taking account of changing traffic conditions. There is, however, a price to be paid for this. A SCOOT system will be more costly than a comparable TRANSYT system for the same signal network. With SCOOT, both the provision of detection loops and their calibration adds to the cost of the system compared with TRANSYT.

For networks where the traffic flow patterns are comparatively stable, for example, a commuter highway network which does not afford a multiplicity of route choice for most work journeys, the advantages of the SCOOT system may not be justified relative to the additional cost. On such networks where the flow can be predicted with some reliability, a conventional UTC system (using TRANSYT) will work well and may be quite adequate. SCOOT will provide greater additional benefits for networks where the flow is least predictable.

However, a balanced view of all matters must be taken, including the requirements for traffic data.

## Safety

Traffic conflicts are separated in time by traffic signal control. There is generally good observance by motorists of traffic signals and thus introduction of traffic signals can lead to increased safety at a junction, for both motorists and other road users, notably pedestrians.

## Checklist

### Isolated traffic signal control junction
- Is it an isolated traffic signal controlled junction (i.e. not linked in operation to another junction)?
- OSCADY used to compute traffic signal timings.
- Control options are:
  - fixed time
  - vehicle actuated
  - MOVA

UTC
- Traffic signals coordinated over an area wide network, so as to minimize overall delays.
- TRANSYT used to compute signal timings, based on historical traffic data.
- SCOOT option operates using dynamic traffic data. Vehicle detectors are required.

### Safety
- Vehicle conflicts segregated by time.
- Pedestrian facilities can be explicitly provided.
- Good observance of signal control. Introduction of traffic signal control can lead to improved safety.

## References

MOT/RRL (1963) Road Note 34, *A Method for Measuring Saturation Flow at Traffic Signals*, MOT.

TRRL (1986) RR67, *The Prediction of Saturation Flows for Road Junctions Controlled by Traffic Signals*, TRRL

Department of Transport (1989) *OSCADY* User Manual, HCSL/R/42, Department of Transport.

TRRL (1987) RR105, *OSCADY: A computer Program to Model Capacities, Queues and Delays at Isolated Traffic Signal Junctions*, TRRL.

TRRL (1980) LR 888, *User Guide to TRANSYT Version 8*, and (1988) AG8, *TRANSYT/9 Users Manual*, TRRL.

Department of Transport (1981) TA 15/81, *Pedestrian Facilities at Traffic Signal Installations*, Department of Transport.
TRRL (1990) AG10, *MOVA Traffic Control Manual*, TRRL.

# Chapter 10
# Road Safety

## General

A proposed development should be designed such that there is no detrimental traffic impact in terms of highway safety. There are two aspects to consider:

- new traffic movements directly generated by the development,
- existing traffic already on the highway network (prior to the development), and which may be affected by the generated traffic and/or the proposed access arrangements.

It is the legal duty of a local authority to promote road safety. Therefore, the highway safety aspects of a submitted planning application are material considerations in determining the application. Further, local authorities are generally committed to realizing a reduction in road accidents. In this regard, there may well be some proposals of the highway authority which are expected to contribute to improved highway safety. Such proposals may be in the form of clearly defined road improvement schemes and/or traffic management measures, or may be more general in the form of policies adopted by council; a development scheme should take account of these matters.

In many cases a development proposal submitted for planning permission includes measures which will result in improved highway safety, compared with the existing situation. In such circumstances, implementation of the development proposals can be expected to result in a net benefit in highway terms.

When a development planning application is refused, there is often a stated reason for refusal which relates to highway safety. This might, for example, be phrased something like: '... to the detriment of highway safety'. It is therefore important that issues of highway safety are fully and carefully considered during preparation of the development proposal.

There are a number of matters which may be relevant in respect of highway safety issues regarding a development, including:

- Geometric details of access proposals. Do these conform with good engineering practice and relevant design standards?
- Accident record of highway onto which additional traffic will be generated by the development. Is there an existing accident problem on the local highway network in the vicinity of the development site?
- Are vulnerable road users, such as pedestrians and cyclists, adequately catered for by the proposed arrangements?
- Buses. Are the proposed arrangements acceptable in terms of bus provision?

## Safety audit

Safety audit is the name given to the design check of a highway scheme, where the objective is to ensure that the design excludes features which may contribute to the occurrence of accidents, as a consequence of circumstances which may reasonably be expected to occur. The procedure followed is to carefully and methodically examine the detail operational characteristics of the proposed geometric arrangements, in respect of all matters of highway safety.

Safety audit of highway schemes is a mandatory requirement of the Department of Transport for trunk roads and motorways. For roads under local authority control the safety audit requirement is at their discretion. However, safety audit of highway proposals is increasingly being required by local authorities.

## Accident records

In the UK the police are responsible for reporting accidents and compiling records, using the form STATS 19. These are a comprehensive set of details of the incident, including: day, date, darkness or light, types of vehicles involved, vehicle manoeuvres involved, age and sex of injured person, severity of injury, weather, road surface condition. The STATS 19 data are restricted to reported accidents that involve personal injury. These data are held by the local processing authority (for example, the police force or county council) and the Transport Research Laboratory (TRL, an executive agency of the Department of Transport).

However, it is widespread practice for local authorities to store the accident data on their own computerized accident database system, designed to hold and present the information in a manner which is most useful to the authority. This may involve a digitized local authority road network. The accident data can then be conveniently downloaded from the computer either in the form of printed output records for each accident, or plotted onto a paper printout of the computer model of the highway network. The accident records for a specified location or length of highway can normally be purchased from the local authority (or its appointed agent). This enables convenient confirmation of whether there is an existing road safety problem in the location of interest to the developer.

The (injury) road accident is defined by the Department of Transport as one involving personal injury on a public highway, including footways, in which a vehicle is concerned. It is only required that an accident be reported when it involves damage or injury to the property or person of a third party. There is, therefore, no legal obligation to report a single vehicle accident when only the driver is injured and/or only his vehicle is damaged. This is one significant reason why accident records represent an under-reporting of road accident totals.

### Injuries

It is usual to classify an accident by the highest severity of casualty incurred as a result of the incident. Therefore, interpretation of the accident record data requires an understanding of the injury categories. There are three categories defined in Great Britain:

- fatal injury: death occurs within 30 days
- serious injury: detention in hospital, however slight the period
- slight injury: no detention in hospital.

## Accident analysis

The initial objective of examining accident record data is to establish whether there is an existing accident problem. If this appears to be the case, it is necessary to delve deeper to try and understand the causal nature of the problem. The purpose of this exercise is to explore whether remedial measures can be proposed, and implemented, which will assist in accident reduction.

For this to be the case, the accidents which occur must be of a 'treatable' nature. That is to say, an accident occurring because of driver heart failure is not an accident which could reasonably be avoided because of measures which the highway authority could implement. Similarly, a vehicle which goes out of control because of mechanical failure is not an accident cause which can be remedied by introduction of highway treatment or traffic management measures. On the other hand, an accident which occurs due to skidding may be avoided in future by suitable remedial highway surfacing treatment.

## Development considerations

The objective is to ensure that the traffic impact of the proposed development does not exacerbate an existing accident problem or create a new one.

Where there is an identified existing accident problem, or concern, it may be that the development proposals can include measures expected to reduce or remove the existing problem. For example, if there is an existing right-turn manoeuvre identified as a road safety problem, the development proposal may include introduction of a right-turn facility to provide for this existing movement. Albeit the development may increase the demand for the right-turn manoeuvre, the net effect can be an improvement in highway safety.

A number of issues may be relevant in respect of the road safety aspect of a development proposal; some examples include:

- speed of vehicles, in relation to existing road geometry
- existing road geometry – does this conform to current design standards?
- right-turn manoeuvre
- junction control, or lack of it
- pedestrians
- bus manoeuvres
- cyclists
- visibility available to drivers
- skid resistance of highway surface.

Further information regarding many of the above points is given in the relevant chapters, including some traffic management measures which may be implemented to effect improvements in highway safety.

## Checklist

### *Existing (pre-development)*
- Is there an existing highway safety problem in the vicinity of the proposed development?
- What do the accident records reveal?

### *Proposed development*
- Consider the vehicle movements generated by the development. Does this include any manoeuvre which seems likely to present a highway safety problem?
- Consider design measures to remedy any potential highway safety problem which may reasonably be considered likely to occur and be attributable to the proposed development.
- Identify measures included within development proposals which will improve the existing road safety situation. This represents a highways benefit of the proposed development.

# Chapter 11
# Public Transport

## General

The potential role of public transport in providing access to developments should not be neglected. Whilst the majority of visitors to many large developments, particularly those in out-of-town locations, arrive by private car, there is nevertheless often scope to provide for public transport travellers, to the overall benefit of the development. This applies for a variety of development uses, including for example retail, office and leisure. Within an established city or town centre location the potential for public transport trips to and from the development may be higher than for other sites.

It is advantageous if the scope for assisting public transport journeys to a development is considered at an early stage of the development project. It may be that simple and comparatively inexpensive details can be incorporated in the development proposal, providing effective measures for assisting public transport travellers.

The modes of public transport available generally comprise bus and rail. In this context the latter is assumed to include light rail schemes.

Although not perhaps generally viewed as public transport, taxis are included within this chapter, as providing a service which can reduce the need for on-site parking spaces and also permit visitors to the development to share the same vehicle.

## Buses

There are a range of facilities which can be provided to assist bus travellers, examples include:

- bus bay,
- bus shelter,
- relocation or introduction of a bus stop,
- bus lane,
- bus only street or length of street,
- bus priority at traffic signals.

At the extreme, a development may include provision of a complete new bus station, for example at a major out-of-town development site.

In considering provision of a bus facility, attention should be given to ensure this meets the requirements of the interested parties, including potential passengers, the local authority and the bus operator.

A bus operator will only elect to provide a new bus service if this is commercially viable. Thus, where a development site is not located on an existing bus route, early discussion with bus operators is helpful in devising a scheme which is likely to support a bus service.

## Rail

In general, there is not as much scope for a development to include measures aimed at assisting rail travellers. This is allied to the infrastructure required for rail travel and the scarcity of existing track compared with roads, and thus also land availability and cost of service provision. For these reasons, rail schemes are outside the scope of the overwhelming majority of developments.

Nevertheless, there are cases of a major development being a catalyst to the introduction of a rail link, recent examples including Meadowhall retail centre (Sheffield) and Manchester Airport. The cost of such rail schemes is great.

However, where opportunity exists for exploiting existing rail infrastructure this should be considered, if judged to be beneficial in terms of providing improved access for development visitors. Examples might be; if there is an existing light rail network capable of extension to serve the development site; potential for introducing an additional station along the existing line, to serve the development.

It is generally only likely that very major development proposals can take on board the financial contribution necessary to introduce or significantly enhance rail facilities.

## Taxis

Increasing consideration is being given to the role of taxi as the mode of travel to and from some developments. For example, many food superstores provide telephones to help shoppers book a taxi when they are ready to leave the store. Some stores provide space on-site for taxi pickup and drop off, or even taxi rank.

It is worthwhile considering whether it is desirable to include taxi facilities within the development.

## Park and ride

Park and ride is the generic name for schemes whereby parking spaces are provided at a site some distance from the desired destination and travellers then complete their journey by public transport. Such schemes can be successful if appropriately designed, and can reduce traffic flows on congested links of the highway network without deterring passenger trips to a development.

The public transport mode can be bus or rail (the latter including light rail). In all cases there are a number of key components for a successful park and ride scheme. These include, for example:

- Site for car parking in an accessible location, offers security for users, is environmentally acceptable and is large enough to cater for demand.
- Public transport service (bus or rail) available from park and ride site. This must be convenient, reliable, frequent and comfortable.
- Demand for central area parking (destination of public transport from park and ride site) exceeds available car parking space.
- Cost of park and ride is favourable compared with single mode car journey.

Bus-based park and ride schemes have been offered for many years, although historically the majority have tended to be of a seasonal nature (for example, Christmas shopping on Saturdays, summer holiday locations). As a good bus service is a key element of any bus-based park and ride scheme, it is crucial to agree arrangements with a bus operator that will provide a reliable service at acceptable cost levels.

In general, rail-based park and ride schemes tend to be aimed at commuters, and may thus be particularly suitable for developments such as offices. The opportunity for rail-based park and ride is obviously dependent upon the availability of rail track, as well as land conveniently adjacent to a rail station site.

In some circumstances it may be advantageous to a development if the proposal includes some contribution to the provision or enhancement of a park and ride scheme. This is most likely to apply to a major town centre development.

## Conclusion

Finally, it is worth noting that enhancement of facilities for public transport users may well be a significant factor when weighing the impact of private vehicle traffic generated by a development. A balanced view of the traffic impact of a proposed development is needed.

# Chapter 12
# Other Traffic

## General

The effects and requirements of the private cars and commercial vehicle traffic associated with developments are considered in some detail within this book. However, this should not be interpreted as implying that the needs of other road users are not important, as this is most definitely not the case. Public transport is addressed in Chapter 11. Similarly, this chapter considers some of the issues relevant to pedestrians, pedal cyclists and the disabled (mobility impaired), when preparing development proposals.

It is stressed that a comprehensive and cohesive approach should be adopted in designing a scheme which considers the needs of all road users. Specifically, where opportunity exists to include at the start of scheme design measures aimed at helping vulnerable road users, without incurring unreasonably high costs, this should be grasped: resulting in an improved final design. Specifically, the needs of pedestrians, pedal cyclists, disabled and others should not be addressed by making token provision, as a bolt-on, at the end of scheme design. With some fore-thought there may be opportunity to provide well designed facilities at little cost, to the benefit of the scheme and the community. Each case must be assessed on the circumstances; the point being made is to consider these issues at the early stages of scheme development and to be aware of opportunities.

## Pedestrians

Pedestrians are the most vulnerable road users and as such their require-ments should be carefully appraised within the context of a development scheme. Generally, at some stage of a trip to a development each visitor will be on foot, irrespective of the mode of arrival at the site. Ideally, the design of pedestrian areas should be an integral part of developing the scheme design and not an afterthought or 'add-on' when the major design parameters are fixed. Similarly, detailed thought should be given at an early stage to the approach routes of pedestrian visitors to a site.

### Development car parks

Developments which generate a significant proportion of vehicle trips generally provide car parking. Examples of such developments include: food superstores, non-food retail stores, hospitals, multi-screen cinemas, bowling, offices.

The design of the car park layout should reflect adequate consideration of the needs of pedestrians. Relevant factors include: conflict between pedestrians and vehicles, and personal security.

### Approach routes

The need for special pedestrian facilities should be considered on approaches to the development. Suitable measures can range from the quite simple to the more comprehensive, examples include: traffic islands, widening of footway, formal pedestrian crossing facility (for example: pelican crossing, dedicated pedestrian stage at traffic signal controlled junction), pedestrianization. (See Chapter 13 for details regarding 'pedestrianization'.)

### Traffic islands

The following relate to the provision of traffic islands:

- width: 1.2 m to 1.8 m, depending upon location. Minor road island generally 1.2 to 1.5 m,
- opening or dropped kerb in the centre, to assist particularly prams and wheelchairs,
- adequate street lighting, including bollards on traffic island
- island in minor road: set back minimum 3.0 m from continuation of kerbline of major road.

### Zebra and pelican crossings

Zebra crossings operate on a priority basis, whereas pelican crossings are controlled by traffic signals. The Department of Transport set down the recommended criteria for requiring a formal pedestrian crossing. These relate to a combination of vehicle flow and pedestrian flow. It is not desirable to introduce a pedestrian crossing which will be underused.

A zebra crossing may be less costly to introduce than a pelican crossing (as the former does not require traffic signal equipment). However, a zebra crossing is not suitable in some circumstances, including:

- high vehicle flows at high speeds,
- locations of continuous pedestrian flow,
- area operating under urban traffic control (UTC), see Chapter 9.

### Pedestrian stage at traffic signals

At a traffic signal controlled junction it may be feasible to include a dedicated pedestrian stage in the signal timings. In this case, special 'green man' designs are included on the appropriate traffic signal heads. Computer analysis of the traffic signal junction will predict the effect that a pedestrian stage will have upon vehicular traffic flows and delays (see Chapter 9).

### Personal security

There is increasing awareness of the need to design a site layout that avoids introducing secluded areas which present pedestrians with a perceived or real threat to personal security.

One such example is in the layout of a residential development. Whilst tree and shrub-lined paths which are not overlooked by dwellings may appear attractive in aesthetic terms, they can provide a threatening aspect to single pedestrians. This is reflected in the current design guidance for layout of roads in residential areas, notably within Design Bulletin 32 (Department of the Environment and Department of Transport, 1992).

Similarly, a development car park should be laid out in a manner designed to avoid unsafe areas for pedestrians, where they may be accosted and the event unobserved.

In respect of observation, there has been increasing use of closed circuit television (CCTV) cameras to assist in security, both at car parks and within developments. Whilst this has a cost, both capital and ongoing operation and maintenance, it benefits visitors in the car park, shopping mall etc., and this can only benefit the development.

## Pedal cyclists

Over recent times there has been increasing awareness of the difficulties faced by (pedal) cyclists; these are among the most vulnerable of road users. The level of accidents to cyclists is acknowledged to be unacceptably high. At the same time it is recognized that cycling provides an environmentally-friendly mode of transport.

There has also been a steady increase in support from local authorities in terms of cyclist provision. Many councils have adopted policies which require consideration to be given to the needs of cyclists. The practical translation of these policies is varied but may include, for example: allocated budget sums for cyclist provision, requirement that all new road schemes and highway improvement schemes must consider including measures to assist cyclists, aspirations to provide a network of cycle routes throughout a local authority. In the latter case the proposed cycle route may be primarily for leisure purposes or a commuter facility. Many local authorities have an appointed officer within the highways department to consider the needs of cyclists.

When preparing a development proposal it is prudent to investigate whether the local authority has any proposals for a cycle route or any other cyclist provisions within the vicinity of the development site. It may be that the development scheme can be designed to include such measures in a manner which does not detract from the proposed development itself. The inclusion within a planning application of measures aimed at assisting cyclists represents an added benefit of the proposed scheme, and a benefit to the community in general.

The measures which may be introduced to assist cyclists are varied but include:

- cycle lane,
- cycle parking,
- special facilities at traffic signal junction,
- toucans (signal controlled crossing which caters for pedestrians and cyclists),
- access route for cyclists when other vehicles are prohibited.

An example of the latter case can occur where it is proposed to 'stop up' a highway and it may be possible to retain a through route for cyclists.

It is essential when considering cyclist provision to consider whether measures proposed will be attractive to cyclists. It is of no use introducing measures which cyclists do not elect to use; this is contrary to the interests of cyclists and others, as well as a waste of scarce economic resources.

## Disabled (mobility impaired)

The special needs of the disabled should be considered within the overall design of a development proposal. There is increased awareness of the difficulties of this sector of the community and a number of measures to assist them are now standard practice. For example: provision of disabled parking spaces within a development car park, conveniently located to minimize distance from car to development (for example, shop, office, cinema); ramps as an alternative to stairs; use of tactile surfacing at points of pedestrian crossing.

It is worth noting that many of the difficulties encountered by the disabled are shared by those with prams. As many development uses can expect to attract a significant proportion of such visitors it is especially sensible to ensure good safe design of pedestrian circulatory areas.

## References

Department of the Environment and Department of Transport (1992), Residential Roads and Footpaths, Layout Considerations, Design Bulletin 32, HMSO, London.

# Chapter 13
# Traffic Management

## Relevance of traffic management techniques to development proposals

Traffic management may be considered as a means of optimizing the available highway network, in accord with specified objectives, which include highway safety and environmental quality. Traffic management is also used as a generic term, which for new works, for example, a new road or car park, can describe measures designed to help accommodate the consequent traffic impact.

The term 'traffic management' comprises a variety of techniques for dealing with traffic and highway related issues. There may appear to be a blurring of the distinction between 'traffic management' and highway engineering generally; in practical terms this is not particularly important. The purpose of this chapter is to concisely summarize the measures which may be considered the tools of traffic management; in many cases the details of such measures are described fully in other chapters herein (for example Chapters 8 and 9, roundabouts and traffic signals respectively). Additionally, included within this chapter is information not presented in other chapters, relating to pedestrianization and traffic calming.

While the initial impression for those of some professions may be that matters described under the umbrella term of traffic management for example, traffic calming or a provision of bus layby, are not particularly relevant to development proposals, this is not so. Such traffic management measures and techniques may be required as an integral part of the design of a development proposal. This is illustrated by two examples.

First, a proposed residential development requires an on-site road layout which takes account of the need to keep vehicle speeds to a minimum in the interests of highway safety. There may also be a need to consider other traffic issues, such as:

- avoidance of the introduction of a 'rat-run' or short cut through an area;

- provision for particular categories of road user such as pedestrians, cyclists and bus travellers;
- avoidance of undesirable levels of parking on the carriageway.

Second, it frequently occurs that the traffic impact on the local highway network of a proposed development is such that some off-site highway works are required. The required works may be relatively simple, such as the introduction of waiting restrictions or provision of a bus layby, or may be more extensive, for example introduction of traffic calming measures on side roads which may otherwise suffer from increased traffic caused by the development.

In both the above examples, there is a need to consider traffic management measures as part of the development proposals. Each case must be assessed on its particular circumstances, and consideration of the need to introduce traffic management measures does not always lead to the conclusion that such measures are necessary as a result of the proposed development.

In any case, it is wise for the developer and/or his representative to have an understanding of the terminology involved in traffic management and the justification for such measures to be required as part of a development proposal, so that discussions with the highway authority may be most productive.

There follows a general statement of the objectives of traffic management, the procedures which should be followed in design of traffic management schemes, identification of common traffic management techniques, and finally a detailed description of two major categories of traffic management measure: pedestrianization and traffic calming.

## Objectives of traffic management

In general terms, the principle aim of traffic management may be described as ensuring the best overall use of the existing highway network and improving highway safety, without impairing the environmental quality. In other words, to make the best use of what is available and to optimize the benefit to the community of the resources offered by the highway network. Traffic management measures may relate to a single traffic category, for example pedestrians or cyclists, or to mixed traffic.

There are usually disadvantages of some sort associated with proposed traffic management measures; it is rare to be able to devise a scheme which has only advantages. For example, an increase in pedestrian green time at a pelican crossing will help the elderly and disabled, but increase vehicle delays. Any traffic management scheme is essentially a compromise, as different categories of road user have different and sometimes conflicting requirements.

The objectives of traffic management measures may be summarized as to:

- be relatively inexpensive and capable of early implementation,
- improve the usefulness of existing facilities, acknowledging the different requirements of different categories of road user,
- improve safety, or as a minimum, maintain the existing level of safety,
- protect the urban environment, improving it where possible.

## Principles underlying design of traffic management schemes

Introduction of a traffic management scheme will result in some change in operation of the highway network. The anticipated degree of change can only be predicted and the actual degree of change be subsequently quantified if the existing situation, prior to implementation of the traffic management measures, is known quantitatively. It is stressed that knowledge of current conditions is essential when considering implementation of measures which may radically affect the operation of the highway network. This is required initially as a basis for deciding whether or not changes should be made, and as an aid in formulating the details of any such changes.

Thus, generally, surveys should be undertaken to establish the present day travel patterns prior to introduction of traffic management measures which may alter these patterns. Survey techniques vary depending upon the data which must be collected. Advice regarding appropriate survey techniques is provided in other relevant chapters. For example, it may be a simple matter of recording existing waiting and loading restrictions or bus stop locations, or it may be necessary to undertake traffic count surveys (see Chapter 5) or parking surveys (see Chapter 14).

## Traffic management techniques

Relatively inexpensive techniques available for developing comprehensive traffic management proposals include:

- one-way streets or systems,
- road-paint measures (for example, lane lines, direction markings, road signs),
- pedestrian safety measures (crossings, guard rails, traffic islands), see Chapter 12,
- on-street parking controls, see Chapter 14,
- improved junction controls (introduction of island and/or priority control, right-turn lane, roundabout, signals), see Chapters 7, 8 and 9,
- linking of traffic signals (TRANSYT, SCOOT), see Chapter 9,
- pedestrianization measures,

- bus priority measures, see Chapter 12,
- cyclist provision, see Chapter 12,
- provision for HGVs (lorry routes, lorry parking), see Chapter 15.

# Pedestrianization

The emphasis of a pedestrianization scheme is on the improvement and safety of the pedestrian environment, rather than the improvement of flow of traffic through an area. This may well be in the interests of a development proposal.

For example, consider the case of an established retail street which has become unattractive to shoppers. It may consequently be proposed that the shop premises are extensively refurbished together, perhaps, with some new buildings. In such circumstances, pedestrianization is likely to significantly increase the future attractiveness of the area to shoppers.

Another example is a development proposal which incorporates the creation of a pedestrianized area within the scheme design; this might be created by new construction or may be achieved by changes to existing access arrangements within a defined area.

When considering pedestrianization a variety of factors must be considered, including: access and servicing requirements, disabled access, bus movements, taxis, alternative routes for diverted traffic. If buses are permitted access to the pedestrianized area, then the arrangements must be clear and laid out in such a manner as to prohibit high speeds.

## Aims of pedestrianization

These may be summarized as to:

- attract people
- provide a sense of place that strengthens community identity and pride
- reduce noise and air pollution
- promote urban conservation
- increase property values and council revenues
- reduce number of accidents

and optionally, to

- create special rights-of-way for bicycles and buses.

## Design objectives

These include:

- continuity
- safety

- comfort (for example, less noise and fumes)
- convenience (footway links between key points in the system should be as short as possible)
- pleasure in walking, improved by the above.

### Alternative forms of pedestrianization

The options comprise:

- *full pedestrianization*: streets are totally paved and all motor vehicles banned at all times,
- *partial pedestrianization*: same as full pedestrianization, except delivery vehicles are permitted limited access, and in some cases buses may be permitted throughout the day,
- *streets with selective traffic bans*: for example, no cars,
- *occasionally pedestrianized streets*: for example, market days.

### Legislation

This is discussed in Chapter 16. There is a choice between using the Town and Country Planning Act 1990 or the Road Traffic Regulations Act 1984.

### Benefits of pedestrianization

A well designed scheme results in:

- users stay longer on visits,
- increased numbers of people regularly visit the pedestrianized area,
- more money is spent by visitors in shops along pedestrianized streets,
- greater economic benefits to provider: increased turnover for shops, increased property and rental values, increased income to local authority.
- greatly increased range of on-street activity.
- large scale seating areas can fulfil the function of a town park within the city centre (for extensive schemes).

## Traffic calming

Traffic calming is a term which has become increasingly and much used in recent years. This may be viewed not so much as a new concept, but rather a wider utilization and enhancement of existing measures, to meet objectives defined by shifting emphasis in the way priority is accorded to different categories of road users. In other words, priority for non-vehicular traffic requires different treatment of roads, (in terms of layout, desirable speed and environmental quality), than is dictated by the objective of maximizing vehicular capacity of a road.

The principle of removal of extraneous vehicular traffic has been widely practised within shopping areas. Traffic calming extends this to residential areas. The concept of the pedestrian having priority within residential areas, and the associated desire for an improved environment, underlies the practice of traffic calming. Although traffic calming is much associated with residential areas, the techniques are also applicable in areas of other type of land use.

The techniques employed under the banner of 'traffic calming' concern control of vehicular traffic to meet safety and environmental objectives. The concept has previously been more widely applied within mainland Europe. As with the term 'traffic management', a precise definition of the term 'traffic calming' is not a key issue. It is, however, helpful to all parties if, in discussions with highway authority engineers and planners, a developer or his representative understands the justification for a traffic calming scheme: this necessarily requires an appreciation of the objectives of traffic calming.

### Relevance to development proposals

If a development is likely to lead to intensification of traffic on streets where such traffic increases are not acceptable, then introduction of traffic calming measures may be appropriate as part of the development scheme, to mitigate the traffic impact of the proposed development. Attention should be given to ensuring that both the volume of traffic and the speed of vehicles are appropriate for the highway.

For example, where the traffic impact of a development proposal is considered to include likely diversion of traffic to existing residential streets, this may well be considered undesirable and inappropriate. In such cases, it may be that off-site traffic calming works (in the affected streets) are included within the development proposal.

In the case of a new residential development, or an extension to an existing development, it may be that incorporation of some traffic calming measures will enhance the development proposal.

### Aims of traffic calming

An underlying objective is to shift the emphasis of priority from vehicular traffic to pedestrians, with concomitant increase in safety for the pedestrian (the most vulnerable road user). Specific objectives may be summarized as to:

- reduce speed of vehicles
- create conditions which encourage 'calm' driving behaviour

- remove extraneous traffic
- enhance the environment: reduce noise and air pollution and improve the visual amenity
- improve safety.

### Techniques used in traffic calming schemes

There are a variety of measures available, including:

- road humps
- speed tables
- cushions
- rumble strips
- 20 mph speed limit
- gateway treatments
- chicanes
- road narrowing/throttles
- footway build out
- central islands
- different surface treatments
- road markings
- landscaping (both hard and soft)
- traffic management measures.

Of these, it is perhaps the road humps, 20 mph speed limit, chicanes and road narrowing/throttles which are amongst the techniques most widely perceived as representing traffic calming.

The objectives of the traffic calming scheme should be carefully defined. For example, achieving reduction in vehicle speeds in the interests of reduced vehicular accidents and increased pedestrian safety. In this case one option is to introduce road humps. However, this can be undesirable on highways with high bus flows, in which case alternative techniques should be considered, such as chicanes.

A well devised traffic calming scheme may comprise several of the elements listed above, but might include only a single measure. It is quality of proposal which is important, not quantity of measures. The objectives must be carefully defined, taking account of the needs of all road users, so that an appropriate and effective scheme is achieved.

# Chapter 14
# Parking

## Need to provide car parking

The car trips generated by a development demand car parking spaces. It is important to provide adequate parking, both in respect of the traffic impact on the local highway network and also for the commercial success of the development.

### Impact on highway network

The consequences of demand exceeding the capacity of the development's car parking provision may include:

- Cars park in inappropriate locations, for example on nearby residential streets which are unsuited to short or long term parking use (other than perhaps meeting the needs of residents).
- Queue of cars waiting for a space (in development car park) may extend onto the highway, causing traffic jams on the carriageway and an associated safety hazard.
- Cars circulating on the adjacent highway network in search of a parking space (either on-street or at another car park). This loads additional traffic onto the highway network, which may increase congestion (for example, Saturday shoppers in a city centre unable to find a parking space circulate on city centre highway network).

### Development needs

If adequate car parking is not provided to meet generated demand, then this can act as a deterrent to potential users of the development. This is illustrated by the example of retail use: if car park capacity does not meet the true demand generated by shoppers, then some potential customers may elect to visit an alternative shopping destination which does afford sufficient and convenient car parking. Similarly, for a city centre office development, if there are insufficient car parking spaces to meet the needs of potential tenants or purchaser, then they may select alternative office accommodation which does meet their car parking requirements.

## Over-provision

It is also important that a development does not over-provide parking spaces. From the viewpoint of the developer, there is no need to incur unnecessary expense. Neither is it in the best interests of a local planning authority to permit a development which includes large paved areas (or multi-storey structures) with car parking spaces exceeding demand. The larger the proposed area of car parking the greater the visual impact. Details of design in matters such as planning and general layout of car parking area, and taking into account factors such as personal security within the car parking area, can become increasingly complex as the scale of car parking provision increases.

It may also be that in some locations a development with spare car parking capacity may attract car trips not generated by the development itself (the car park being in a location attractive for other destinations). While this is not likely to be of benefit to the development itself, the local planning authority may in some circumstances view this as a benefit. The developer must carefully weigh the costs of providing additional car parking spaces (beyond meeting the needs of the development) against the general parking space requirements of the local authority.

There is another aspect of over-provision of car parking space which may be considered by the local planning authority, in some locations and circumstances. The availability of car parking capacity in a convenient location can act as an inducement to use a car rather than an alternative such as bus. This latter issue may need to be considered in the light of a council's policy in respect of public transport (for example, if it is council policy to discourage car trips and encourage use of buses).

## Commuted sum payments

Situations arise where a local authority requires more car parking provision than can be provided on the development site. The developer may negotiate with the local authority to achieve a relaxation in the requirement, to a level of parking provision that it is possible to provide on-site. If this can not be achieved, one alternative is for the local authority to accept that the shortfall of parking, which can not be accommodated on-site, be provided elsewhere by the developer.

Another possible option, which has been accepted and indeed promoted by some local authorities, is the concept of commuted sum payments for parking. This is where the local authority accepts a payment from the developer (£x per space of parking shortfall) to enable the local authority to provide additional car parking in another location which they consider acceptable.

### Summary

It is in the interests of all parties that development proposals include the right amount of parking provision to cater for the traffic generated by the development use.

## Car parking standards

Many, but not all, local authorities have adopted standards of development car parking space requirements (which may be published). These vary according to the development use, recognizing that different uses generate varying levels of traffic and consequently varying levels of car parking requirement. There is no single set of standards adopted by all local authorities, and early consultation is recommended to determine the level of car parking provision the local authority desire for a particular development.

The level of local public transport provision can influence the modal split of people's trips to the development. Thus, for example, the parking standards of a local authority within a conurbation may vary from those in rural areas.

In the past, where there has been disagreement between developer and local planning authority on car parking requirement, there has in many cases been a tendency by the local authority to err on the side of a higher car parking space requirement. This is perhaps for the reasons discussed earlier in this chapter (in respect of the consequences of under-provision for operation of the highway network). In some cases this has been a crucial factor in determining a development planning application; there are examples of refusal of planning permission with insufficient car parking cited as a reason for refusal, in some cases being the prime reason for refusal.

However, concern has been growing amongst many local authorities that a development providing car parking is contributing to a sustained increase in car traffic on the highway network. Many local authorities are carefully reviewing the attitude to development car parking provision alongside other policies which affect the general quality of the environment and the consequences of pursuing policies which result in an ever-increasing need for additional roadspace. This is particularly true in large urban areas which are centres of employment. Such considerations include the question of public transport provision, and issues such as park and ride are increasingly coming to the fore (see Chapter 11).

Therefore, the situation may arise whereby a local planning authority wishes to restrict the number of car parking spaces provided by a development, for example so as not to encourage additional car trips into the central business area. This may be particularly true in the case of generated commuter car trips, and thus may apply more to certain types of development use than others.

A central area office development is an example where a local authority may conclude that provision of significant development car parking is likely to act in conflict with council policy of encouraging public transport use and discouraging commuter traffic from the central area highway network. However, the developer may hold the view that without the proposed development car parking being permitted, the offices will not be attractive to potential purchasers or tenants.

In general, it is advisable that local authority car parking standards form the starting point for considerations of development car parking requirements, but that these are not imposed in an undesirably rigid and inflexible manner. It should be recognized that in many cases, for example a large county, the application of car parking standards may benefit from some consideration of local mitigating factors.

Where a local authority does not publish development car parking standards, there is a particular need to consider carefully the observed local conditions and operation at similar existing developments.

### Examples of car parking standards

As explained, for a given development use there is no single standard of car parking requirement which is universally applied. However, Table 14.1 provides examples of typical car parking standards which have been used by a number of local authorities. It is stressed, however, that enquiries should be made of the relevant planning authority when considering a proposed development. Equally, it is important to consider the parking requirements as indicated by marketing research and advice.

## Parking surveys

Empirical data of observed car parking operations is widely used as the basis for estimating the car parking requirements of different developments. This can be particularly helpful where, for a proposed development, there is some site specific doubt as to the veracity of application of the car parking standards of a local authority. In such circumstances observed parking characteristics of similar developments in similar locations can provide useful comparisons.

For some developments it may be appropriate to consider the level of car parking space availability over an area wider than the development site itself. Such an example may be for a city centre rail or office development. This can provide some indication of whether the proposed car

**Table 14.1**   Car parking space requirements: typical values for types of development.

| Type of development | Typical car parking space requirement |
| --- | --- |
| *Residential*<br>Typical family<br>accommodation | Range:<br>2 space/dwelling (driveways may count; may include<br>garage deemed as one space)<br>up to<br>4 space/dwelling (garages excluded) |
| *Office*<br>Central area locations | Range:<br>1 space/250 square metres GFA, down to providing for<br>operational needs only |
| Non-central locations | 1 space/25–50 square metres GFA |
| *Shopping*<br>Food retail | 1 space/20–9 square metres GFA (e.g. higher<br>requirement for food superstore) |
| DIY | 1 space/15 square metres GFA |
| *Industrial* | 1 space/65–25 square metres GFA |
| *Hotel* | Residents and visitors:<br>1 space/bedroom (maximum), plus additional for public<br>areas (refer below, e.g. restaurants) |
| *Restaurants/bars/club* | Visitors:<br>1 space/2 seats, or<br>1 space/10–5 square metres GFA |

*Notes:*
The car parking space requirements noted are *typical* values, or range of values. These vary between local planning authorities.

In all cases, the desired car parking space requirements of the local planning authority should be ascertained. These can be assessed for reasonableness against the requirements of other local planning authorities and of known developments operating satisfactorily.

In some cases, a developer may require car parking spaces in excess of the stated requirement of the local planning authority.

parking is likely to be superimposed upon a situation of over- or under-supply of car parking in the proximity of the development site.

In some cases a local authority may view favourably, or indeed have a stated desire, for a development to provide parking spaces beyond those required by the development itself. An example of this might be a proposed local district shopping development, comprising two or more units totalling perhaps some 20 000–30 000 square feet (approximately 2000–3000 square metres). In such a situation, where the proposed district shopping centre is located astride or near to the local high street, if there is an existing identified shortfall in parking supply, a local authority may view the proposed development as offering an opportunity to increase car parking space. This may be a matter on which the developer is prepared to assist, in the interests of achieving a negotiated planning permission for the development proposal.

In such examples as given above, it is necessary to have a quantitative understanding of existing car parking in an area which extends beyond the boundary of the development site itself.

Car parking information is collected by survey, the method depending upon the level of information which is required. The types of car parking survey may be broadly classified as:

- parking supply (availability)
- parking concentration
- parking duration

### Parking supply survey

This is a survey of existing facilities, which fall into three categories:

- off-street space inventory
- on-street space inventory
- street regulations inventory.

The information resulting from the survey can be marked onto a suitable scale plan of the area, perhaps scale 1:1250, thereby providing a convenient visual reference.

The type of information to be collected varies depending upon the level of detail needed for the specific project purpose, but may include some or all of the following.

*Location and control*
- On-street
  - kerbside, parallel, oblique, etc.
  - capacity (actual count if marked spaces, otherwise estimated based upon available space).
- Off-Street
  - number of spaces provided
  - type, e.g. ground level only, multi-storey, underground
  - private or public ownership and use
  - entry and exit locations
  - size of area
  - open space, covered.

*Time restriction*
Restrictions by time of day and duration of permitted/excluded parking, e.g. parking for 40 minutes only, return prohibited within 1 hour.

*Charging policy*
- ○ free, charged
- ○ method of collecting parking fee
- ○ scale of charges, including conditions such as time
- ○ special arrangements, e.g. contract parking, operational parking
- ○ enforcement measures.

From the parking inventory and details of restrictions, an evaluation can be made of the theoretically available space-hours of parking. This can assist in estimating potential car parking revenues and assessing alternative charging strategies (although this must be considered alongside parking demand information and other relevant factors).

### Parking concentration (accumulation) survey

This survey determines the actual number of vehicles parked at a given time at all locations (on- and off-street within the survey area).

Note that the 'survey area' may be restricted to a single off-street car park. In such a case, the concentration survey can be undertaken in the following manner:

- define survey time period, from start to end time, (e.g. 0800–1800 hours),
- define survey time blocks, say 15 or 30 minutes, (e.g. 0900–0930, 0930–1000, etc.),
- count the number of parked vehicles at the commencement of survey period,
- record vehicle arrivals and departures over the survey period (for each defined time block),
- count number of parked vehicles at end of survey period (as check on observed data).

For each time block, the number of observed arrivals minus departures gives the net increase in cars parked, compared with the preceding time block. Thus the number of cars parked at any time is known (for each time block). An example of the results of a parking accumulation survey, (carried out as described above), at a single multi-storey car park are presented in Table 14.2.

### Parking duration survey

This survey quantifies the length of time spent by vehicles parked in the study area.

**Table 14.2** Car park accumulation survey.

| Time | In | | Out | | Accumulation[1] | %[2] Occupancy |
|---|---|---|---|---|---|---|
| | No | %[2] | No | %[2] | | |
| Before 1000 | | | | | 908 | 53 |
| 1000–1100 | 589 | 35 | 202 | 12 | 1295 | 76 |
| 1100–1200 | 625 | 37 | 351 | 21 | 1569 | 92 |
| 1200–1300 | 502 | 30 | 431 | 25 | 1640 | 96 |
| 1300–1400 | 477 | 28 | 471 | 28 | 1646 | 97 |
| 1400–1500 | 560 | 33 | 473 | 28 | 1733 | 102 |
| 1500–1600 | 538 | 32 | 591 | 35 | 1680 | 99 |
| 1600–1700 | 275 | 16 | 595 | 35 | 1360 | 80 |
| 1700–1800 | 70 | 4 | 650 | 38 | 771 | 45 |
| After 1800 | | | | | 191 | 11 |

*Notes:*
Typical findings from a Saturday survey for a city centre car park (i.e. reflects shopper car parking demands).

(1) Design capacity 1700 cars
(2) Percentage of 1700 space capacity.

## Patrol survey

The patrol survey technique can be used to collect both concentration and duration data simultaneously, in other words, parking usage data.

The survey area is defined and then divided into sections of a size which can be toured every half-hour (or other suitable time interval; it might be 1 hour, or even 15 minutes if rapid turnover is anticipated). The area may be patrolled on foot. In some circumstances it may be appropriate to patrol by another mode (for example car or bicycle).

Registration numbers are noted on each patrol tour. These can be either directly written down, or recorded using a hand-held tape recorder or hand-held electronic data capture device. In the case of tape recorded data this must later be transcribed, and the electronic data capture device may require down-loading onto a suitable office based machine. A further method is to use a video cassette recorder (VCR), loaded in a car and driven around the survey area; data can be subsequently analysed.

Generally, the simplest and easiest method to organize is the foot patrol, with registration numbers either written down directly or recorded onto tape recorder, and this is suited for many survey situations. It is generally the larger scale survey over an extensive study area which requires the more sophisticated survey methods.

The parking usage survey data can be analysed to obtain a variety of information relating to the survey period. This includes items such as:

- total number of vehicles parked (over whole survey period),
- total number of vehicle-hours of parking,
- the percentage of total vehicles parked during a given time period,
- the percentage of vehicle-hours of parking in a given time period,
- parking accumulation in a given time period.

### Direct interview

This is the most expensive and comprehensive of the parking surveys. Motorists are interviewed at their place of parking and questioned concerning their origin, destination and trip purpose, as well as estimated duration of parking.

For on-street parking, the interviewer is allotted a specific survey length. In a city this would not normally exceed say 100 m kerbside.

For off-street parking, the interviewer is stationed at the vehicular entrance, or exit, of the car park. If interviews are planned at the entrance to the car park, consideration should be given as to whether this may cause a queue of vehicles to form at the entrance to the car park. This may result in interference to traffic flow on the highway network and may deter some motorists from using the car park (they elect to park elsewhere rather than wait in a queue attributable to the interview surveys). In the latter case, this gives rise to a distorted record of parking demand pattern at the car park.

The information recorded in an interview survey may include:

- registration number (for identification purposes),
- vehicle classification: car, taxi, heavy goods vehicle (HGV), etc.,
- nature of parking: legal, illegal, kerbside, off-street, etc.,
- time at which vehicle stopped (i.e. arrives at parking location),
- time at which vehicle started (i.e. departs parking location),
- last point at which the driver made an essential stop, (i.e. origin of this journey),
- driver's destination after leaving the parked vehicle,
- purpose of the stop (i.e. parking requirement): work, shopping, business, off-loading, leisure, etc.

Note that for an interview survey in an off-street car park it may be necessary to have an additional survey team member recording the registration number and time of vehicles departing the car park, in order to ascertain actual parking duration.

### Suppressed parking demand

If the parking space supply (availability) exceeds parking demand, then the survey methods described above record the true parking demand.

However, if the parking supply is less than demand, then only an indication of the true demand can be obtained by survey. Suppressed vehicle demand refers to those vehicle drivers not willing to attempt to find a spare parking space in an area with scarce spaces. An example of this is when the selection of a shopper's destination is critically influenced by the type and availability of car parking at the alternative destinations considered.

### Parking measurements

There are a number of terms used in reference to measures of parking. These include:

- *Parking accumulation*   Number of parked vehicles in an area at a specified time. Integration of the parking accumulation curve, over a specified period, determines the parking load, in vehicle-hours per specified time period.
- *Parking occupancy.*   $\dfrac{\text{vehicle accumulation}}{\text{total number of spaces.}} \times 100\%$
- *Parking volume.*   Defines the number of vehicles involved in a parking load (i.e. vehicles per specified time period).
- *Parking duration.*   Time a vehicle spends parked.
- *Parking turnover.*   Rate of use of parking spaces (i.e. for a specified time period).
- *Parking index (PI).*   Used to assess relative amounts of parking at a particular location.

If $p_1$ = number of vehicles parked

$p_2$ = number of spaces available

Then   $PI = \dfrac{p_1}{p_2} \times 100\%$

- *Space hour occupancy.*   $\dfrac{\text{total time parked by all vehicles}}{\text{duration of survey} \times \text{number of spaces.}}$

## Car park layout

Whilst the majority of development parking provision tends to be for cars, there may be a requirement for spaces for other vehicle types. Examples include: a significant amount of goods vehicle parking spaces required at a motorway services area, coach parking at a leisure development, operational parking requirements for goods vehicles and coaches.

Vehicle dimensions vary, between classes of vehicle (say, car and goods vehicle) and even within a vehicle category (for example, not all cars are

**Table 14.3**  Typical parking space requirements: surface vehicle parks.

| Vehicle type | Car | Light van | Coach | Heavy goods vehicle | |
| --- | --- | --- | --- | --- | --- |
| | | | | Rigid | Articulated |
| Vehicle dimensions (m) | $3.8 \times 1.7^{(1)}$ $5.0 \times 2.0^{(1)}$ | up to $6.0 \times 2.1$ | up to $12.0 \times 2.5^{(2)}$ | up to $11.0 \times 2.5^{(2)}$ | up to $16.5 \times 2.5^{(2)}$ |
| Allocated parking area (m) | $4.8 \times 2.3$ | $5.5 \times 2.3$ | $14.0 \times 3.5$ | $14.0 \times 3.5$ | $18.5 \times 3.5$ |
| Overall space/parked vehicle, square metres, including access and manoeuvring space | 20 to 25 | 20 to 30 | 100 to 150 | 100 to 150 | 150 to 200 |

*Notes:*
(1) Typical range of dimensions.
(2) Maximum dimensions normally permitted in UK.

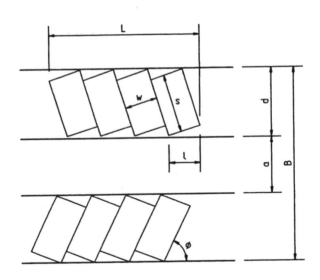

N.B. For 90° parking: l=w, d=s

| | | | |
| --- | --- | --- | --- |
| L | Bay size | d | Stall depth |
| B | Bin width | a | Aisle width |
| w | Stall width | l | Aisle length/stall |
| s | Stall length | φ | Parking angle |

**Fig. 14.1**  Parking layout dimensions.

the same size). Table 14.3 includes typical dimensions for different vehicle categories, together with the associated typical space required for parking, providing a comparison between the parking space requirements for different types of vehicle.

Terms used to describe parking layouts are illustrated on Fig. 14.1 and include:

Stall   floor area intended to be occupied by one parked car
Bay     gap between fixed obstructions occupied by one or more stalls
Bin     width occupied by parking aisle and its adjacent parking
Aisle   strip of floor area which gives immediate access to stalls.

Typical recommended parking dimensions for cars, for various parking angles, are included in Table 14.4.

## Control systems and charging policy

In general, when a development provides car parking this is intended for development-associated use. It may or may not be an objective to achieve profit from operation of the car park. This depends very much upon the nature of the agreements relating to its control and operation.

There are a number of reasons why some form of control system may be required for a development car park. These include:

- desire to generate revenue from car park,
- to deter car parking not associated with the development itself,
- to prevent vehicles entering the car park when it is full,
- security,
- to restrict times of use of car park.

It is possible to control a car park without introducing a concomitant charging policy. This may, for example, be achieved by having a locked chain at the car park entrance, which is removed at certain times (for access), or a barrier system which can be controlled by an operator or pass-card.

A charging policy may be required at a car park to meet financial objectives. The criteria for choice of a tariff system are that it should:

- be capable of collecting all fees
- provide maximum security against fraud
- be easily understood
- be easy to maintain
- be capable of operation in all circumstances.

There are a number of systems currently available.

**Table 14.4**  Recommended parking dimensions: angled parking.

| Parking angle (°) | Aisle width | | Bin width* (stall length 4 m) | | |
| --- | --- | --- | --- | --- | --- |
| | Minimum (m) | Preferred (m) | Stall width (m) | Minimum (m) | Preferred (m) |
| 90 | two-way aisle 6.95 | two-way aisle 6.95 | all | 16.45 | 16.45 |
| 90 | one-way aisle 6.00 | one-way aisle 6.00 | all | 15.50 | 15.50 |
| 80 | 5.25 | 5.25 | 2.3 | 15.404 | 15.404 |
| | | | 2.4 | 15.439 | 15.439 |
| | | | 2.5 | 15.474 | 15.474 |
| 70 | 4.50 | 4.70 | 2.3 | 15.000 | 15.200 |
| | | | 2.4 | 15.069 | 15.269 |
| | | | 2.5 | 15.137 | 15.337 |
| 60 | 3.75 | 4.20 | 2.3 | 14.277 | 14.727 |
| | | | 2.4 | 14.377 | 14.827 |
| | | | 2.5 | 14.477 | 14.927 |
| 50 | 3.50 | 3.80 | 2.3 | 13.734 | 14.034 |
| | | | 2.4 | 13.863 | 14.163 |
| | | | 2.5 | 13.991 | 14.291 |
| 45 | 3.50 | 3.60 | 2.3 | 13.470 | 13.570 |
| | | | 2.4 | 13.612 | 13.712 |
| | | | 2.5 | 13.752 | 13.853 |

*Notes*
* Bin width is for an aisle with a stall on each side.
Recommended stall dimensions (UK) are:

| | |
| --- | --- |
| stall length | 4.75 m |
| stall width | |
| long stay | 2.30 m |
| general | 2.40 m |
| short stay | 2.50 m |
| disabled persons | |
| minimum | 3.20 m |
| preferred | 3.60 m |

### Automatic fixed charge system

This may not be compatible with policy objectives; a low charge produces low income (and may encourage long-stay use) and a high charge discourages short-stay use.

### Fee collection by attendant

Usually a ticket is issued to the motorist from a machine at entry to the car park. Upon leaving, the attendant charges the appropriate fee. If a fixed charge system is in operation, the attendant may be stationed at the entrance.

The advantages of this system include:

- attendant available for advice or if there is a machine fault, and may provide some element of perceived security
- change can be given
- suitable employment for the disabled.

Disadvantages include:

- rate of exit is slow (for pay-at-exit), or rate is slow (for pay-at-entry)
- usually revert to fixed charges at night (in consideration of cost of employing staff throughout the night)
- may be difficult to recruit suitable staff
- Attendants may act fraudulently.

### Pay-and-display system

The motorist is required to estimate length of stay at car park, place appropriate fee into a ticket dispenser (usually on foot after parking vehicle), and is issued with a ticket which must be displayed in the vehicle's window.

If the pay-and-display system is to be effective, it must be clear to car park users that:

- It is an offence to overstay or not pay at all.
- There is a high chance of being detected if in breach of conditions.
- The penalties are sufficient to discourage 'taking a chance' and flouting the system.

Thus the system must be clearly signed and be regularly patrolled by inspectors. Infringements must be pursued if the penalties are to represent an effective deterrent. A sizeable manpower commitment can be required.

Advantages of the system include:

- barriers not required (capital cost item)
- less likely to result in restricted entry and exit to car park
- easily understood
- inspectors may reduce the risk of theft, vandalism and personal security threats
- if machine is full or faulty, the motorist can use another.

Associated disadvantages include:

- Income may be less than with some other systems.
- Unexpired tickets can be (illegally) transferred to an incoming vehicle.
- Correct change is commonly required by machine.
- Upon arrival, motorist required to estimate accurately the maximum length of required stay (to determine fee payable).

### Fully automatic control systems

A variable charge tariff system may be implemented. This can help meet both financial and policy objectives, for example, to encourage high turnover short-stay parking and discourage long-stay parking.

A binary coded ticket is issued at the entrance. Payment may be either pay-at-exit or pay-on-foot. In the former the point of payment is at the exit barrier, approached in the vehicle. In the latter case, (pay-on-foot), paystations are located at convenient points of pedestrian flow and payment must be made before return to vehicle for departure. For pay-on-foot, a ticket acceptance unit is still required at the exit to ensure that a driver has paid the appropriate fee.

Advantages include:

- facilities for change often available
- high degree of security
- staffing costs reduced.

Disadvantages may include:

- expensive to install and maintain
- rate of exit can be slow with pay-at-exit
- clear instructions are necessary for unfamiliar motorists, particularly for pay-on-foot.

# Checklist

### Need to provide car parking
- If the car parking capacity provided does not meet the demand generated by the development use, then
  - cars that queue or circulate in search of a parking space may detrimentally affect the operation of the local highway network,
  - visitors to the development may be deterred, with consequent loss of business.
- The number of car parking spaces required by a local authority for a development can vary according to current council policies; for

example, if a council wishes to discourage car trips into the central area of a city and encourage a modal transfer to bus. Are there any council policies which may affect the car parking requirement?

- If a development site can not accommodate all the car parking required by the local authority, a commuted sum payment may be accepted in respect of the on-site deficit. This enables the local authority to provide the shortfall in parking elsewhere, off-site.

### Car parking standards
- Check if the local authority has adopted car parking standards. If not, check the 'custom and practice' within the authority for the development use in question.

### Parking surveys
- Surveys of similar developments in locations of a similar type can provide a good guide as to the likely requirement for car parking. Check if such data are available.
- The parking survey can collect all or some of the following information:
  - Parking supply (availability): How many vehicles can be parked in the survey area? What regulations, restrictions, charging policy, etc. apply?
  - Parking concentration: How many vehicles are parked in the survey area at a specific time (e.g. 1030–1100 hours)?
  - Parking duration: How long do vehicles stay parked?

### Car park layout
- Typical dimensions for parking spaces are shown in Tables 14.3 and 14.4.

### Control systems and charging policy
- Is revenue required from the car park?
- If so, decide upon method of control (taking account of capital, running and maintenance costs, as well as issues of security).
- Select preferred charging policy. The criterion may be to maximize revenue or to encourage/discourage certain types of user.

# Chapter 15
# Service Vehicles

## General

All developments require some level of access for service vehicles. However, in general it is the large vehicles which require special provision, both in respect of the access route (including junctions) and the parking and loading space provision. In some cases, there is a minimal requirement for access by large vehicles, for example where the main demand is limited to refuse vehicles. However, in other cases the demand for service vehicle access is extensive and can indeed predominate in respect of access and parking requirements. Examples of this include a food distribution centre, (for example, as established by some large food superstore operators) and an industrial trading estate. The level of provision by developments for service vehicles depends upon a number of factors, including size and frequency of vehicles and potential conflicts with other road users.

## Size of vehicle

The size of vehicle is a major determining factor in the space requirements for manoeuvring and parking. Another important factor is whether the large vehicle is rigid bodied or articulated. The maximum dimensions currently permitted for heavy goods vehicles (HGVs) in the UK are summarized in Table 15.1.

## Turning manoeuvres

The geometry of the highway network on the approach route to the development site should be able to accommodate the physical manoeuvres of large vehicles. Of particular concern is the swept path of HGVs as they undertake turning manoeuvres, both on the highway and within the site.

The swept path of a turning HGV does not follow a simple curve. Compound curves should therefore be used on corners to assist turning

150

**Table 15.1** Maximum permitted HGV dimensions: UK standards.

| Vehicle type | Axles[1] (number) | Maximum weight[2] (tonnes) | Maximum length (metres) |
|---|---|---|---|
| Rigid | 2 | 17.00 | |
| | 3 | 24.39 | |
| | 4 | 30.49 | 11.0 |
| Motor vehicle and drawbar-trailer | 4 or more | 32.52 | 18.35 |
| Articulated | 3 | 24.39 | |
| | 4 | 32.52 | |
| | 5 or more | 38.00 | 16.5 |

*Notes*
(1) Normal maximum axle weight is 9.2 tonnes. This may be increased to 10.17 tonnes or 10.5 tonnes, (for the sole driving axle of 2-axled motor vehicles), if wide or twin tyres are used.
(2) Dependent upon axle spacing.

Maximum height is not generally specified. The exception is articulated vehicle with 5 or more axles: maximum height of 4.2 m.
Maximum width is generally 2.5 m. Refrigerated vehicles maximum width is 2.58 m.

manoeuvres (as illustrated in Fig. 15.1). The geometry provided at corners should be designed so that the following are avoided:

- path of turning HGV crossing over into the path of the opposing traffic stream,
- HGV running over the kerb and footway, with consequent structural damage and safety hazard to pedestrians.

General practice is to consider the swept paths of a standard 'design vehicle', to establish the geometry required to accommodate HGV manoeuvres. The Freight Transport Association (FTA) have developed a specification for such a design vehicle which caters satisfactorily for the majority of turning HGVs, and publish (for their members) corresponding space requirements for typical turning manoeuvres. Such swept path layouts can be overlaid onto a proposed design layout, to ensure that HGV turning requirements are adequately met. There are also commercially available computer programs which predict the paths described by large vehicles as they manoeuvre.

At the design stage, consideration should be given to whether there is a realistic requirement to provide for both articulated and rigid vehicles. In general, articulated vehicles are more manoeuvrable than the equivalent sized rigid vehicle (because the radius of the inner swept path described by the rear axle is less); however, generally articulated vehicles tend to be longer than rigid vehicles.

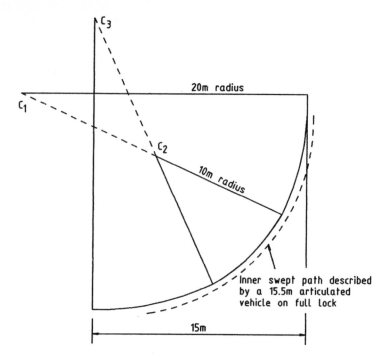

**Fig. 15.1** Compound curve for corners.

## Turning areas

A turning area must be provided at the end of all cul-de-sacs and other locations where HGVs are likely to need to turn around. The reversing manoeuvre for an HGV is more hazardous than for cars, as the rear vision is very restricted. It is therefore preferable that an HGV can turn without the need to include a reversing manoeuvre. This can be achieved by the

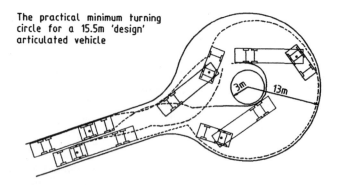

**Fig. 15.2** Circular turning area.

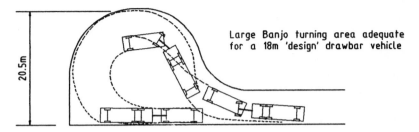

20.5m

Large Banjo turning area adequate
for a 18m 'design' drawbar vehicle

**Fig. 15.3**  Banjo turning area.

circular or banjo forms of layout, as illustrated in Figs. 15.2 and 15.3 respectively. If the necessary space for these manoeuvres cannot be accommodated within the development area, then the alternative of a T (hammerhead) turning area must be considered (as illustrated in Fig. 15.4).

Consideration of the examples of turning areas included in Fig. 15.2–15.4 illustrates that it is essential to keep the defined HGV turning area free of parked vehicles and other obstructions. This requires good management practices at the development, for example particularly within the service areas of shopping developments where 'illegal' parking of cars can be a problem if not adequately controlled.

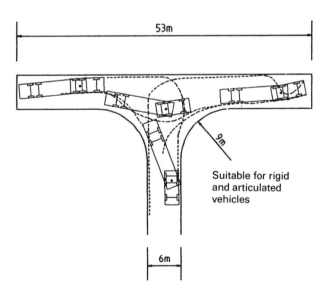

53m

9m

Suitable for rigid
and articulated
vehicles

6m

**Fig. 15.4**  T-turning area.

## Parking

Parking provision for service vehicles must be adequate both in number and location of spaces. Some developments operate strictly controlled delivery systems, for example where delivery vehicles are allotted time slots and entry to the service area is controlled. This can be essential within developments which have a considerable delivery vehicle demand which results in full utilization of the service vehicle area space capacity over significant periods.

Recommended layouts for HGV parking bays are illustrated in Fig. 15.5, with recommended bay width of 3.5 m. Where rows of HGV parking bays are needed it is preferable if the bays are angled at 45° towards the point of egress. Such a layout permits reduced aisle widths (compared with 90° parking bays), thereby maximizing the number of parking bays which can be provided on a given area of land. This may be critical for some development sites, but not others.

## Loading areas

Off-street loading areas for service vehicles are preferable. This avoids unnecessary conflicts between service vehicles and other road users.

Some loading bay layouts are included in Fig. 15.6; recommended loading bay dimensions are included in Table 15.2.

Careful consideration is required to determine the number of loading bays required by a development. Relevant factors include the expected frequency of deliveries and the management regime which is to be operated within the loading area.

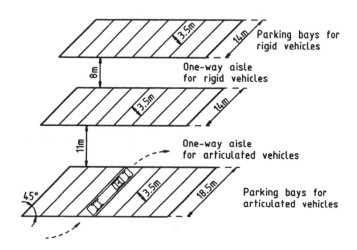

**Fig. 15.5**  HGV parking layouts.

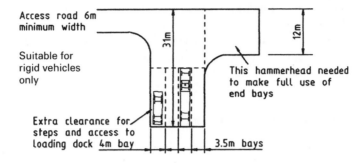

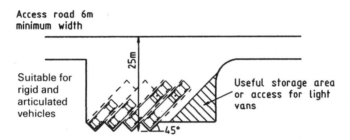

**Fig. 15.6** HGV loading bays.

For example, if unrestricted access by service vehicles is permitted within the loading area, then a greater number of loading bays is likely to be required than if the loading area operates under a controlled and regulated access management system. Some developments operate strict time-controlled delivery systems, with delivery vehicles allocated time slots and entry to the service area managed and controlled accordingly.

## Headroom

Where HGV loading and parking areas are under cover, adequate vehicle headroom must be provided. As the maximum height of HGV is likely to

**Table 15.2** Loading bay dimensions for HGVs.

| Vehicle type | Bay dimensions (m) | |
|---|---|---|
| | Width | Length |
| Rigid | 3.5 | 12.0 |
| Articulated | 3.5 | 17.0 |

# General

Circumstances occur in which, as part of or consequent upon a development proposal, changes are to be introduced in respect of the permitted use of the public highway. For example, where it is proposed to introduce one-way working along an existing length of two-way road; or where it is proposed to 'stop-up' an existing highway. Where such changes are to be introduced, these must be the subject of legal procedures.

# Highway: definitions

A highway is a way on which people have the right to pass and repass, and this public right may be carried out on foot, horseback or by vehicle. This applies in England and Wales; in Scotland the term 'road' is used rather than 'highway'. The following definitions apply:

- *Footpath* – a highway on which the public have the right of way by foot only.
- *Footway* – a way within a highway which also includes a carriageway, and on which the public have right of way on foot only.
- *Bridleway* – a highway on which right of way is by horseback and on foot only.
- *Cycleway* – a way with right of way on pedal cycles, constituting a highway over which the public have right of way for the passage of vehicles.
- *All-purpose highway* – the public have right of way on foot and with vehicles and a bridleway use.

# Traffic Regulation Orders (TROs)

Traffic Regulation Orders (TROs) are made under powers provided to highway authorities (and some other authorities). TROs *cannot* be made by developers or their legal representatives. Thus, if a development's

158

planning permission is conditional upon the implementation of a TRO, there is a possibility that the planning permission may not ever by implementable. The TRO must be approved by the relevant local authority committee and confirmed by the council. At best, implementation is dependent upon the timetable of the highway authority in proceeding with the TRO, once it has been confirmed by the council.

Therefore, it is generally not to be recommended that a development proposal proceeds with integral dependency upon implementation of a TRO. However, it can be quite acceptable for the developer to agree, by negotiation, to contribute to highway works, some or all of which may require a TRO. The key point is that the planning permission should not be conditioned upon the implementation of the TRO.

### Objectives of Traffic Regulation Orders

TROs are made to control the movement and/or waiting of vehicles for a variety of reasons, as set out in the Road Traffic Regulations Act 1984. The reasons include:

- safety
- assisting traffic flow (traffic including any modes, not only vehicular)
- to restrict movements by particular classes of traffic
- to preserve or improve amenity of the road.

### Procedures

The promoting authority must follow a set procedure:

- *Consultations*:   must take place with the police, highway authority (if not the authority making the Order) and organizations representing those affected. Those consulted may include local residents and businesses, as well as emergency services, and organizations representing pedestrians, cyclists, motorists, bus, freight. The extent of consultations varies between authorities.
- *Notices*:   must be placed in the local press and *London Gazette*, setting out the proposals and inviting objections. At the same time, notices must be placed in prominent positions at the site, for a minimum of 21 days. The relevant documentation and plans must be available for inspection by the public. The promoting authority must consider all objections.
- *Objections*:   If the authority decides to proceed with the Order despite receiving objections, then objectors must be informed in writing and notices placed in the press. The chief officer of the Police must also be notified.

   If a TRO prevents vehicular access to property for more than 8 hours in any 24 hours, the conditions to be fulfilled are particularly strict. If an owner/occupier of an affected property objects to the TRO and does not withdraw the objection, then the Order must be confirmed by the Secretary of State.

Temporary orders have no public right of objection.

- *Make the Order:*  provide appropriate traffic signs and road markings.
- *Validity of Order:*  may be questioned up to six weeks after it is made, on the grounds that it is outside the powers of the authority, or that the interests of the applicant were prejudiced by failure of the authority to follow the specified procedure. The Order can not be questioned in law after the six week period.

### Duration of TRO

A TRO can be:

- *Permanent.*
- *Temporary.* Up to three months in areas outside London, but extendable with the consent of the Secretary of State. If a longer period is required it is prudent to make the application to the Secretary of State at the earliest opportunity. If the Secretary of State refuses to extend the Temporary Order, the council must not grant a second closure for at least three months. (Temporary Orders have no public right of objection.)
- *Experimental* (up to 18 months). Experimental Orders follow a different, shorter, procedural system.

Any Order can be revoked at any time.

### Exemptions

These may be incorporated within the Order for certain classes of vehicle, for example buses, pedal cyclists, emergency vehicles.

### Types of Traffic Regulation Order

A variety of measures are introduced on to highways by TRO, some of the most common being:

- one-way streets,
- prohibition of classes of vehicle,
- specified exemptions (e.g. 'except buses'),
- control of specific turning movements: these can be restrictive (e.g. 'no right turn') or mandatory (e.g. 'all traffic must turn left'),

- prohibit waiting at any time, or to restrict waiting at certain times and days of week and limit length of stay.

Note that the following regulatory signs do *not* require a TRO: stop, give-way, keep left or right.

## Stopping up and diversion of highways

When it is required that a highway be 'stopped up', (ceasing to be available for public use as a highway), this is generally achieved using the powers of either the Highways Act 1980 or the Town and Country Planning Act 1990.

## Highways Act 1980

The ways in which an order for the stopping up or diverting of a highway can be made under the Highways Act 1980 are outlined in the following.

### Section 14: Highway (Highway Authority Powers)

This provides for the making of orders authorizing a highway authority to stop up or divert a highway.

### Section 116: Highway (Magistrates Court)

Alternatively, the highway authority can apply to a magistrates court, on the grounds that the highway is either *unnecessary* or that it can be diverted to become *more commodious* to the public.

Conditions or procedures which apply to a Section 116 application include the following:

- Can *only* be made by the highway authority.
- It does not apply to trunk or special roads.
- Any person who uses the highway, or any person who could be aggrieved by the making of the Order, is entitled to make representations at the hearing of the application. This includes the statutory undertakers' authorities.
- Except where the Order relates to a highway accepted to be unnecessary, no part of the highway may be stopped up until the alternative highway has been completed to the satisfaction of the magistrate.
- The Order may provide for the stopping up of the highway for all traffic, or in the part to be stopped up may require the maintenance of a footpath or bridleway.
- If the highway being the subject of the application is not a classified road, advance notice of the intended closure must be provided: in

England, to the district council and the parish council (or the chairman of the parish meeting); in Wales to the community council. If such a body gives *refusal of consent* within two months of notification, the application *cannot* proceed; such refusal of consent is an *absolute bar*.

- The Order must be accompanied by a plan.
- Cost of necessary relocation of plant of statutory undertakers is incumbent upon the highway authority.

## Section 117: Highway (Ask Highway Authority to Apply to Magistrates Court)

Any private individual (including a company) can ask the highway authority to act on their behalf to apply to the magistrates court for stopping up of a highway. It is entirely at the discretion of the highway authority as to whether they accede to the request. If the highway authority decides to proceed, the Section 117 applicant may be required to meet any costs incurred by the authority (in pursuing the application for stopping up or a diversion of highway). If the highway authority declines the Section 117 application, there is no right of appeal, and no one other than the highway authority can initiate proceedings (by the magistrates' route).

## Section 118: Footpaths and Bridleways (Stop Up)

This provides for the stopping up of footpaths and bridleways. To be satisfied that it is expedient for a path or way to be stopped up, the council should be satisfied that it is not needed for public use. Account must be taken of the effect of the Order upon any adjacent land. The Secretary of State will order a public inquiry if there are objectors. A confirmed Order is known as a 'public path extinguishment order' and should contain a map showing the affected length of path.

## Section 119: Footpaths and Bridleways (Divert)

This provides for diversion of footpaths and bridleways. The owner, lessee or occupier of land crossed by a footpath or bridleway (excepting trunk road or special road) must satisfy the council that a shorter or more commodious route is proposed; the council may then make the Order. If unopposed, the Order can be confirmed by the council; if opposed, confirmation is required from the Secretary of State.

## Section 120: If public path in more than one council

If the land ownership for the stopping up or diversion of a public path is located within two or more council boundaries, each council must notify the others of its intentions and each council has to stop up or divert its own section by agreement.

# Town and Country Planning Act 1990

The provisions within the Town and Country Planning Act 1990 for the stopping up of a highway are outlined in the following. In all cases, an Order cannot be confirmed unless there is a valid planning permission. If there are objections from the local authority, statutory undertakers or any other person appearing (to the Secretary of State) to be affected by the Order, and the objection is not withdrawn, a local inquiry should be held. Following the local inquiry, the Secretary of State can confirm the Order, with or without modification, or refuse to confirm the Order.

### Section 247: Highway

This gives the Secretary of State for Transport (and in Wales the Secretary of State for Wales) the power to stop up or divert any kind of highway, if he is satisfied this is *necessary to enable development to be carried out in accordance with a planning permission*. An unambiguous example of this is where the proposed development includes building over an existing highway.

The responsibility for making orders lies with the following:

- Secretary of State for Transport: orders which involve vehicular highways (including the footways of such highways),
- Secretary of State for the Environment: orders concerned exclusively with footpaths and bridleways.

The applicant may be a highway authority, local authority, statutory body, or any other person or company that is competent to undertake the necessary works and procedures. If the applicant is not the highway authority, it is desirable that the application is supported by them (and that there is a letter from the highway authority stating their support in principle).

There is no requirement to state the grounds for making the Order. However, the Secretary of State *must* be satisfied that either:

- a suitable alternative right of way has been, or will be, provided, or
- that such provision is *not required*.

A Section 247 Order may provide for the provision or improvement of other highways. In making an Order the Secretary of State may require any other authority or person specified in the Order to pay or make a contribution to the cost of doing any work required or referred to in the Order.

The proceedings may be concurrent with the process for the compulsory acquisition of land required for the highway to be stopped up or diverted.

## Section 253: Highway (Anticipation of Planning Permission)

This allows the Secretary of State, in certain circumstances, to process a stopping up or diversion order prior to and in anticipation of the granting of a planning permission. However, the Order *cannot be made* until the planning permission is granted.

The Section 253 procedure can be followed where a planning application has been submitted for a proposed development and either:

- The application is made by the local authority or a statutory undertaker or by British Coal, or
- The application is referred to the Secretary of State, or
- The applicant has lodged an appeal with the Secretary of State (under Section 78 of the Act) against a refusal of planning permission or approval required under a development order, or against a condition of any such planning permission or approval.

Other circumstances in which the Secretary of State may act under Section 253 (in anticipation of planning permission) are where:

- The development is being undertaken by the local authority, statutory undertaker or British Coal, and authorization is required by a government department, (and the local developer has applied to the department for that authorization and also requested a direction that planning permission be deemed to be granted for the development).
- A county council, metropolitan borough, London borough or district council certify that they are proceeding with the necessary action to enable them to obtain planning permission for the proposed development.

## Section 257: Footpath or Bridleway (Stop Up: Land Affected by Development)

This allows a local authority to stop up footpaths and bridleways if satisfied this is required to enable development to be carried out, and there is a valid planning permission. Conditions can be attached which require the provision or improvement of another footpath or bridleway.

### Section 251: Footpath or Bridleway (Stop Up: Land held for Planning Purposes)

If land has been acquired for planning purposes and is held by a local authority, the local authority may order extinguishment of rights of way over a footpath or bridleway.

### Section 249: Extinguishment of Vehicular Rights

A local authority may resolve to adopt a proposal to improve the amenity of part of their area. Where this area includes a highway an Order can be made to extinguish the existing vehicular rights, under Section 249 of the Town and Country Planning Act 1990. The Order may include provisoes in respect of:

- particular types of vehicle
- particular persons by whom or on whose authority vehicles may be used
- timing of particular purposes.

The local authority consults the highway authority and any other relevant authority.

The Section 249 procedure is particularly useful for implementing a pedestrianization scheme. It also allows for partial pedestrianization: whereby some vehicles are permitted access at specific times. If vehicles are still physically able to gain entry to a Section 249 pedestrianized area, (for example in the case of partial pedestrianization) there is increased danger that the vehicular entry restrictions will be disobeyed. Therefore, it may be necessary to also implement a TRO which creates relevant offences, to support in law the intention of the Section 249 Order. This then enables the prosecution of those entering by restricted vehicle the area covered by the Section 249 Order.

## Land ownerships and road closure or diversion

Once a road closure has taken effect, the rights of the public to use the highway are destroyed. The 'top layer' of the highway becomes the property of the person (or his successors) on whose land the highway was constructed. If the land was specifically granted to the highway authority for highway purposes, it may revert to the grantor if the land is no longer used as a highway.

A private right of way over what was a public right of way will not be affected by road closure or diversion.

Written consents are required from all of the owners of the sub-soil of the highway to be stopped up or diverted. Application for stopping up or a diversion can be made to the Secretary of State even if written consents have not been received from all affected owners of sub-soil. However, even if an Order is made, it can not be implemented without the necessary written consents, and hence progress of the development may be 'at ransom'.

## Choice of Act for stopping up or diversion

Table 16.1 provides a comparative summary of the provisions within the Highways Act 1980 and the Town and Country Planning Act 1990, in respect of stopping up or a diversion of highways. The Highways Act permits only the highway authority to make the application for stopping up or a diversion. Any objectors to the Order can be heard at the magistrates court. Under the Town and Country Planning Act, the developer can apply directly for an Order to be made. In the event of objection, the Secretary of State decides if a local inquiry is to be held.

## Checklist

### Traffic Regulation Order (TRO)
- TROs are made by the highway authority: a TRO application can not be made by a developer.
- A TRO is made to control the movement and/or waiting of vehicles.
- A developer has no control over the making or implementation of a TRO. It is therefore undesirable for planning permission for a development to be conditioned upon a TRO.
- It is better to negotiate with the highway authority, so that the developer contributes to any highway works which are required as part of or as a consequence of the development, but that the making of any TROs is not a condition of implementation of the planning permission.
- Examples of measures introduced by TRO include: one-way street, waiting restrictions, prohibition of classes of vehicle.

### Stopping up and diversion of highways
- Choice of Highways Act 1980 or Town and Country Planning Act 1990

### Highways Act 1980
- Only the highway authority can apply for the Order.
- To be stopped up the highway must be unnecessary; to be diverted the alternative must be more commodious.
- With applications to the magistrates court, objectors can make representations at the hearing.
- If the district council or parish council (England) or the community

**Table 16.1** Stopping up or diversion of highways: Highways Act 1980; Town and Country Planning Act 1990.

| Act | Highway: Stop up or divert | | | Footpath or bridleway | | | |
|---|---|---|---|---|---|---|---|
| | | | | Stop up | | Divert | |
| | Section | Makes order | Special conditions | Section | Makes order | Section | Makes order |
| Highways Act 1980 | 14 | Highway authority | | 118 | Local authority | 119 | Local authority |
| | 116 | Magistrates court | • Only highway authority can apply.<br>• Highway must be *unnecessary* or diverted to be *more commodious*<br>• Objectors have right to be heard. | | | | |
| | 117 | Magistrates court | • Third party requests highway authority to apply.<br>• At discretion of highway authority; no right of appeal. | | | | |
| Town and Country Planning Act 1990 | 247 | Secretary of State | • Must be necessary to enable development to take place.<br>• Must have planning permission.<br>• Must demonstrate suitable alternative, or that provision not required. | 251 | Local authority | 257 | Local authority |
| | 253 | Secretary of State | • Order can be processed in *anticipation* of planning permission<br>• Order can not be made until planning permission granted. | 257 | Local authority | | |

council (Wales) refuses consent to the magistrates court application (for highway stopping up or a diversion), this is an absolute bar to the Order.

- Footpaths and bridleways: application referred to Secretary of State if there are objectors.

### Town and Country Planning Act

- Must be valid planning permission for Order to be confirmed.
- Application to Secretary of State.
- Must be necessary to enable development to be carried out. One way of being sure of this is by 'building over' the highway to be stopped up.
- Application can be made by developer (as well as highway and local authorities and statutory bodies). Advisable for application to have letter of support from highway authority, if they are not making the application.
- Application can be made in anticipation of permission in some circumstances (e.g. applicant is local authority or applicant has lodged appeal against refusal of planning permission). Even if successful, the Order cannot be made until the planning permission is granted.
- Extinguishment of vehicular rights: Section 249 is widely used to implement pedestrianized schemes.

### Land ownerships

- After road closure, the 'top layer' of the highway becomes the property of the person on whose land the highway was constructed.
- Written consents required from all owners of sub-soil of the highway to be stopped up or diverted: the Order cannot be implemented without these. Applicant should be aware of potential ransom situation.

# Index